AF606866

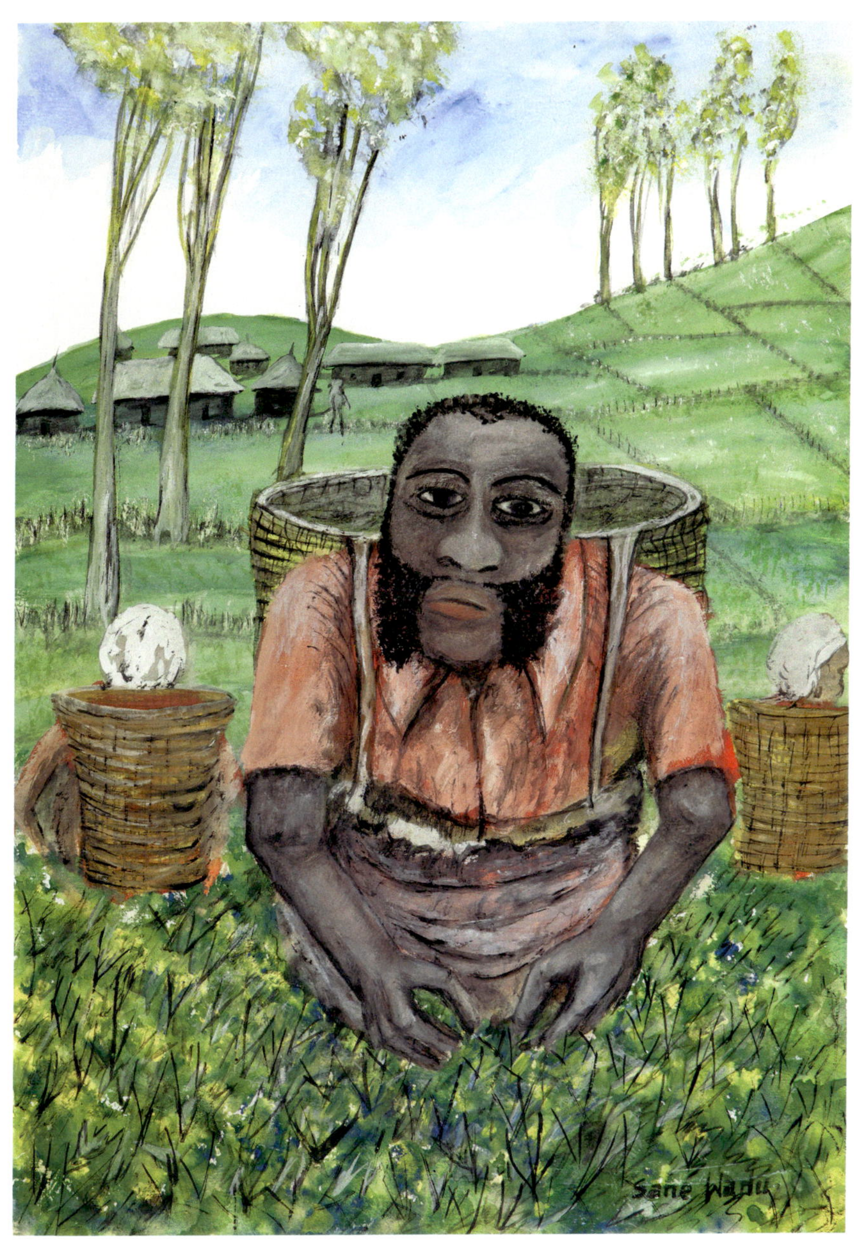

1 Picking Tea

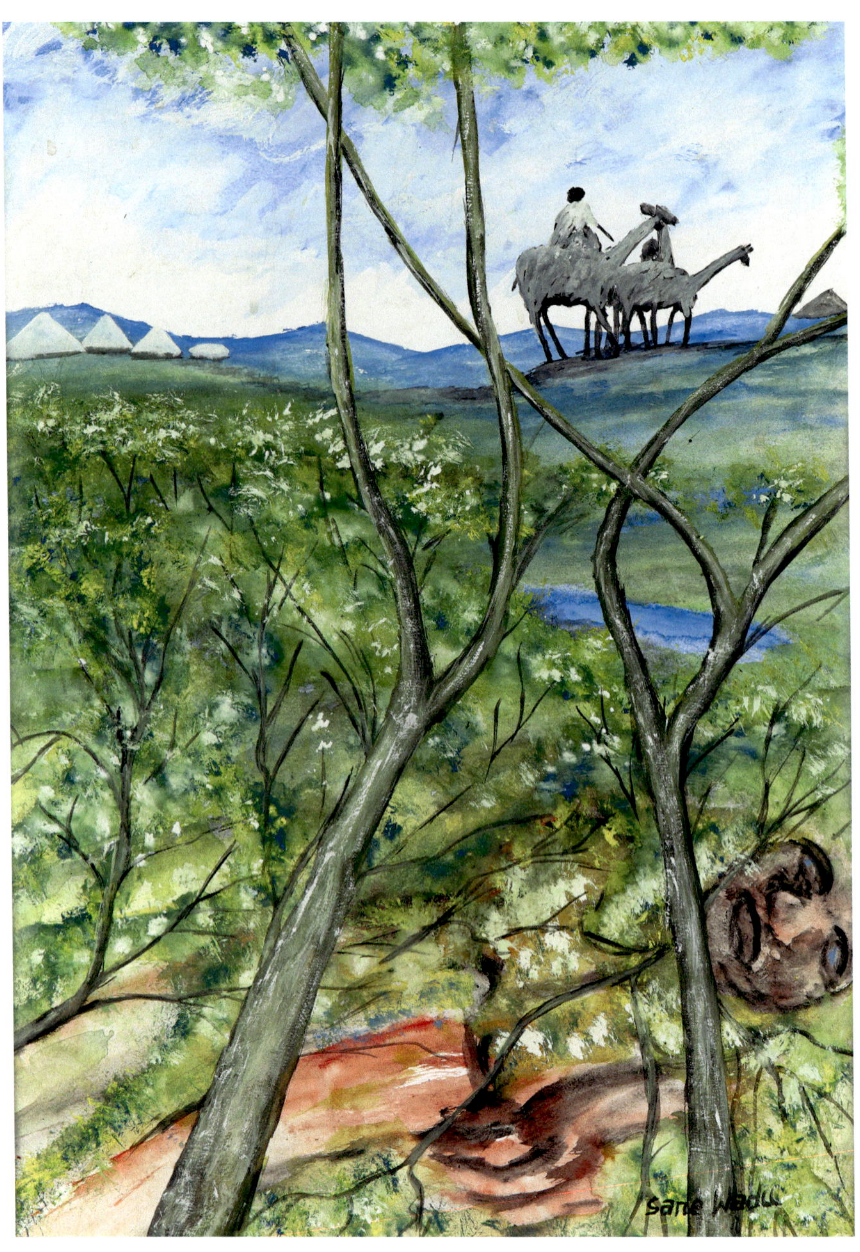

 Lying in Trees *and* A Single Mother   *following spread* Broken Calabash

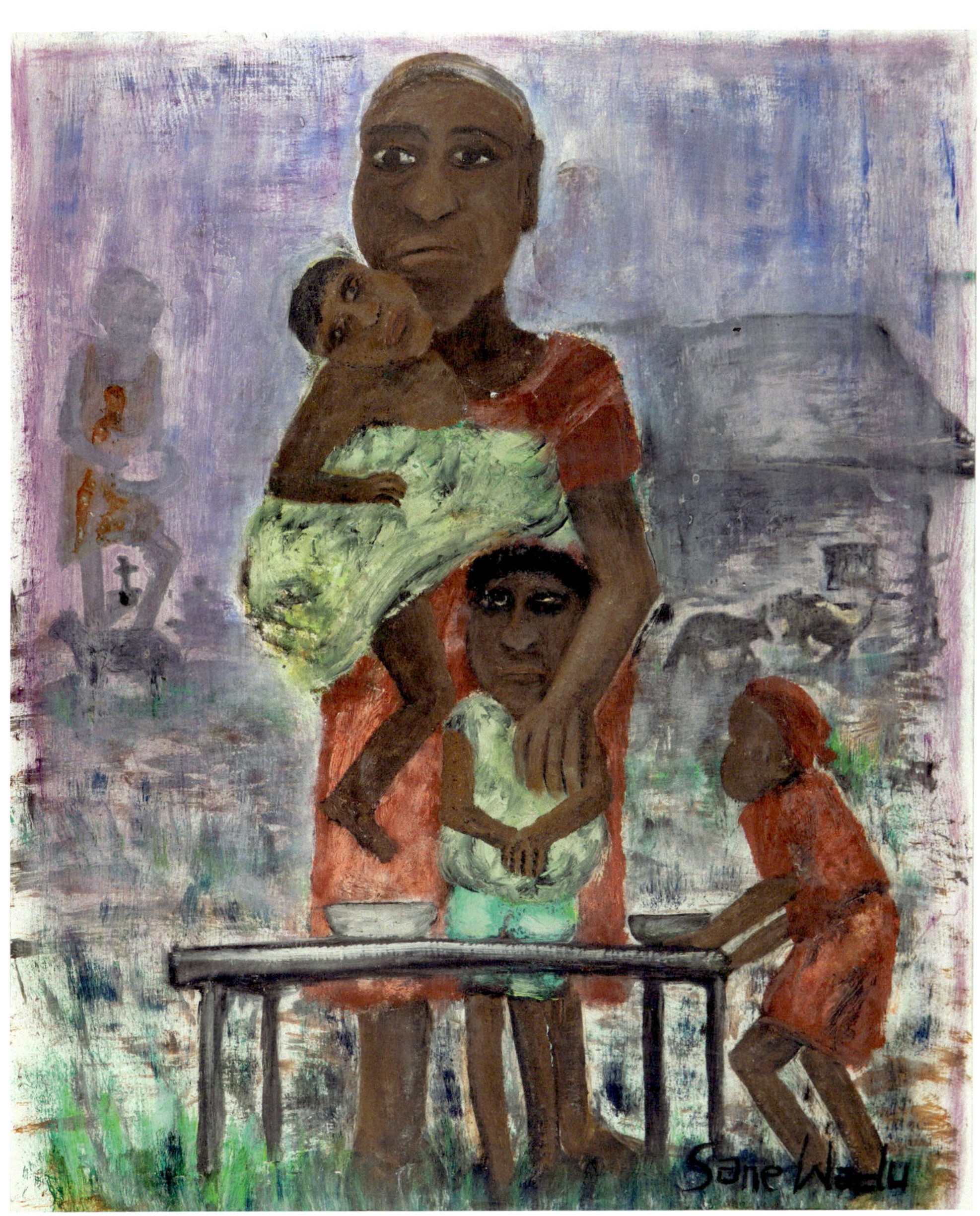
Sane Wadu

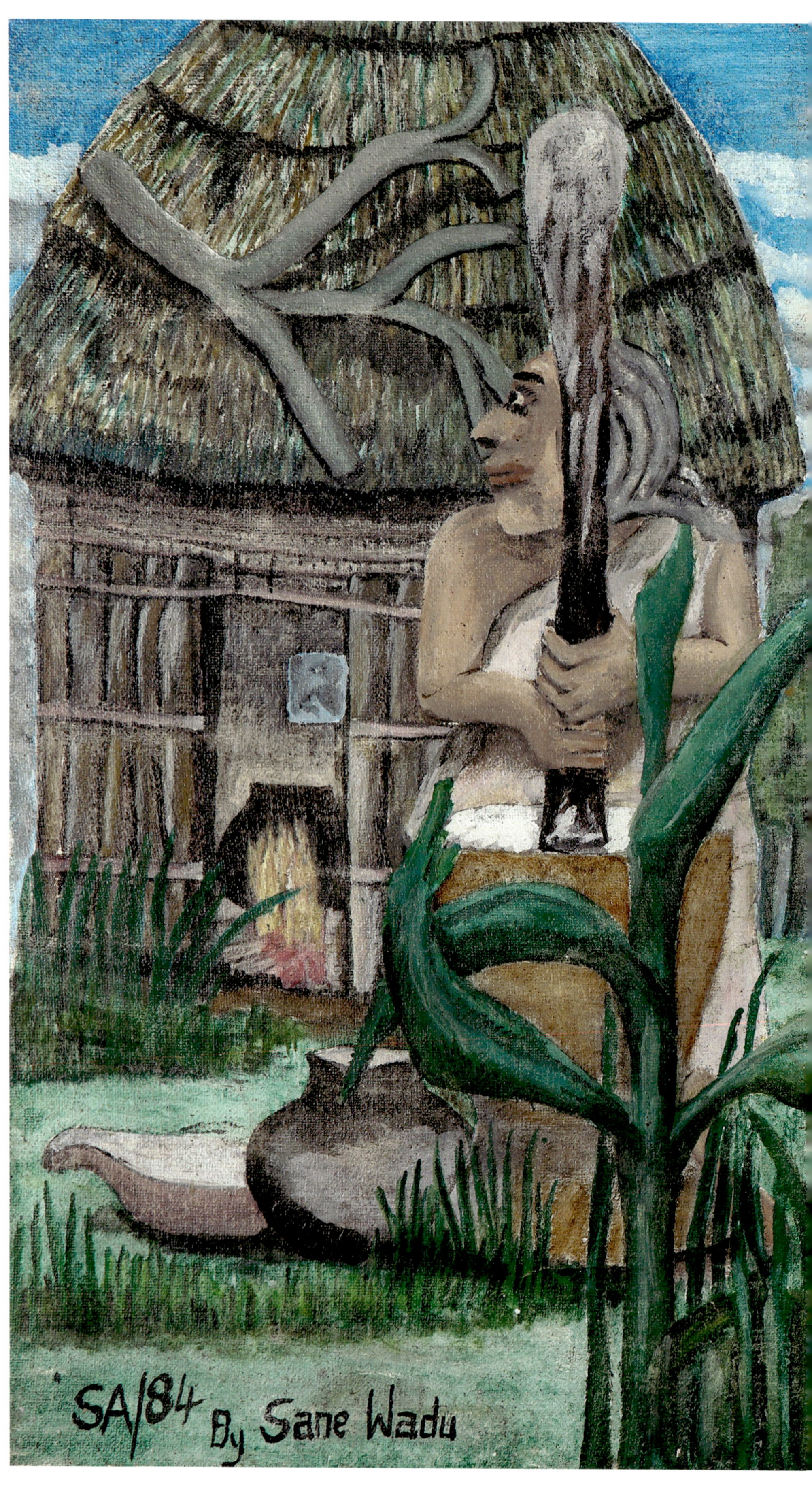
SA/84 By Sane Wadu

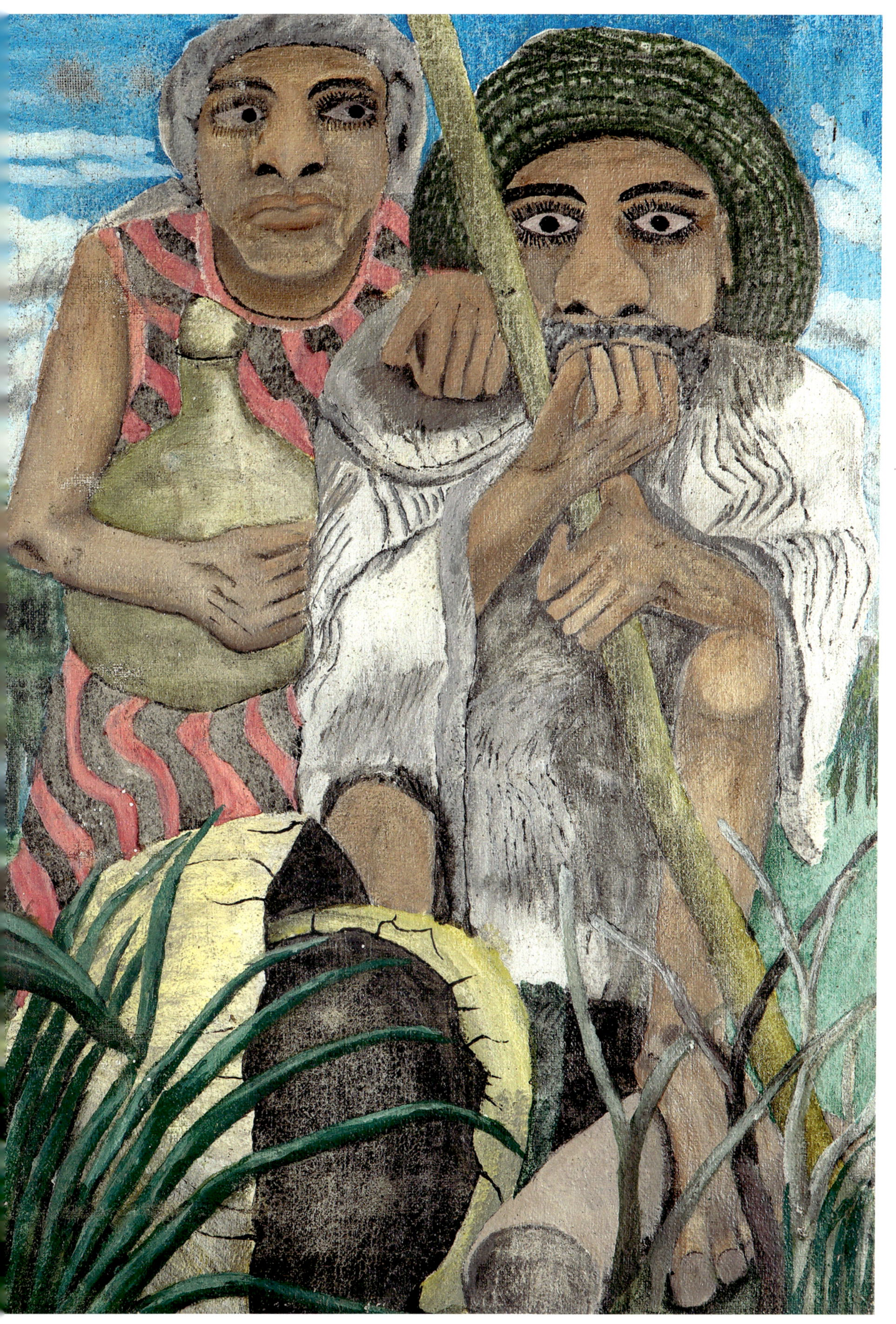

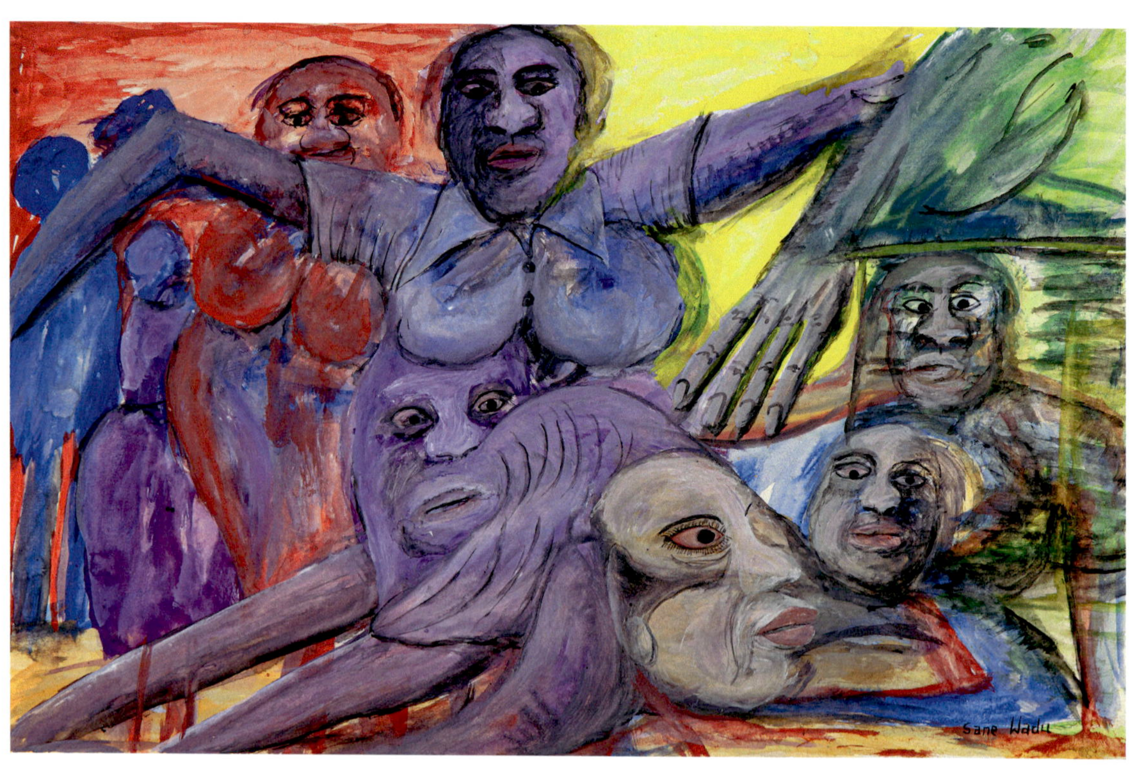

6 Mother Dragon *and* Hopeless Future

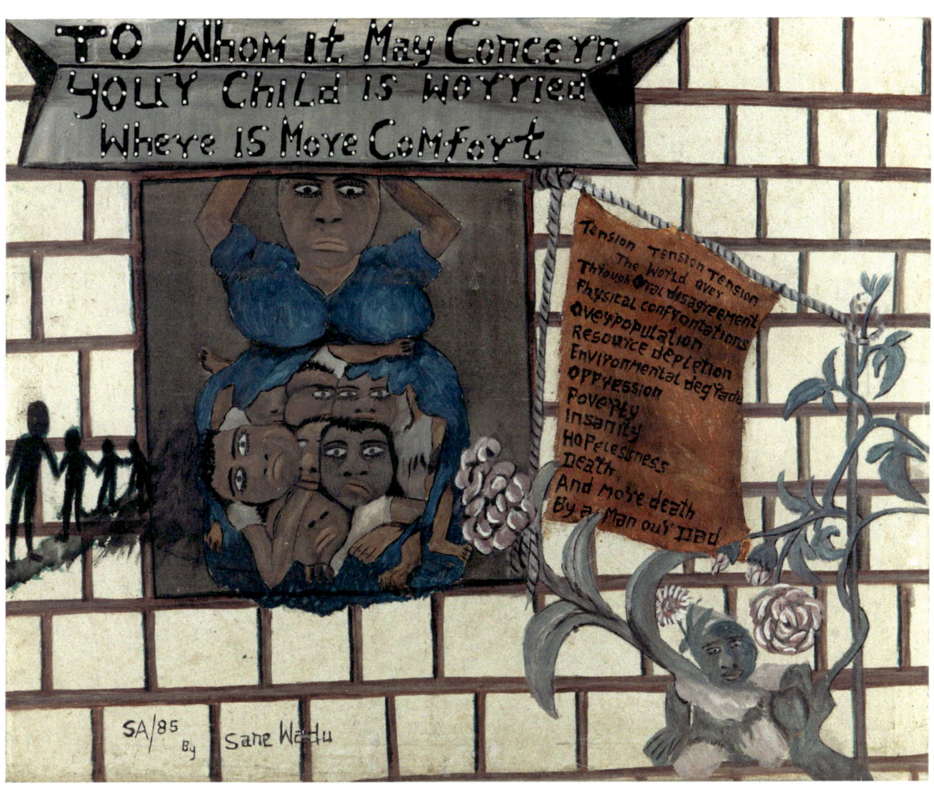
TO Whom it May Concern
Your Child is worried
Where is More Comfort
Tension Tension Tension
The World over
Through Oral disagreement
Physical confrontations
Overpopulation
Resource depletion
Environmental degrade
Oppression
Poverty
Insanity
Hopelessness
Death
And more death
By a Man our Dad
SA/85
By Sane Wadu

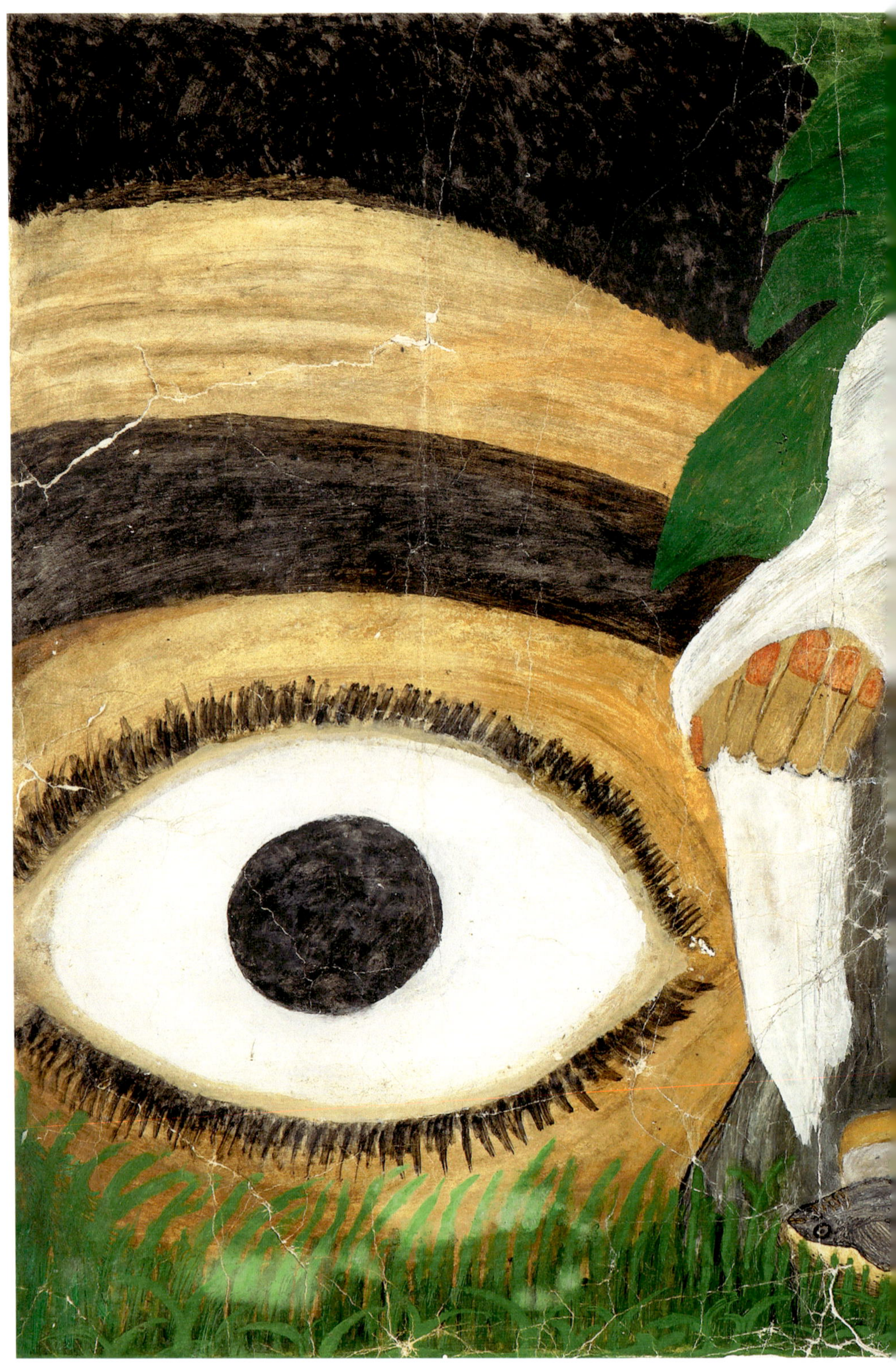

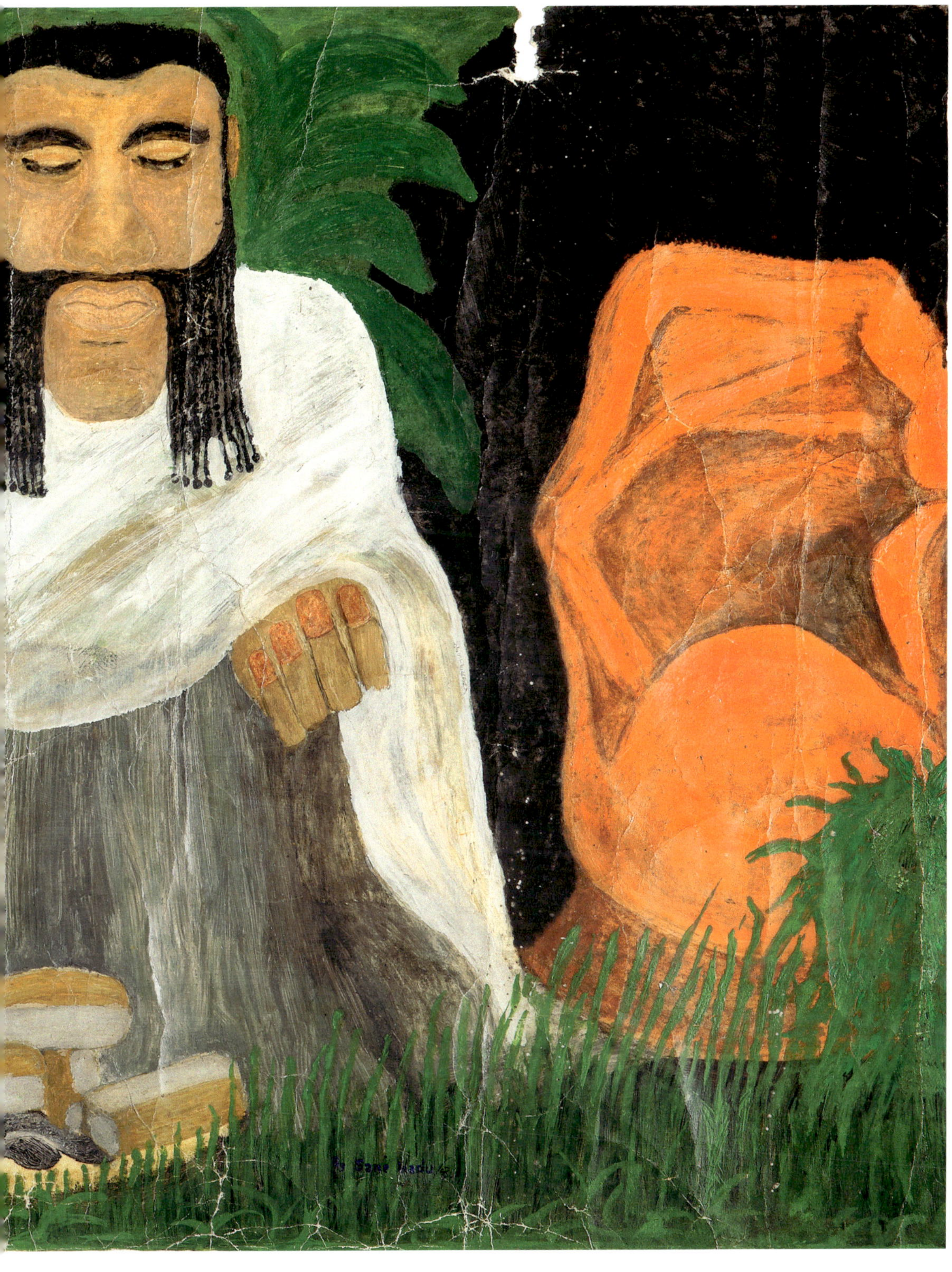

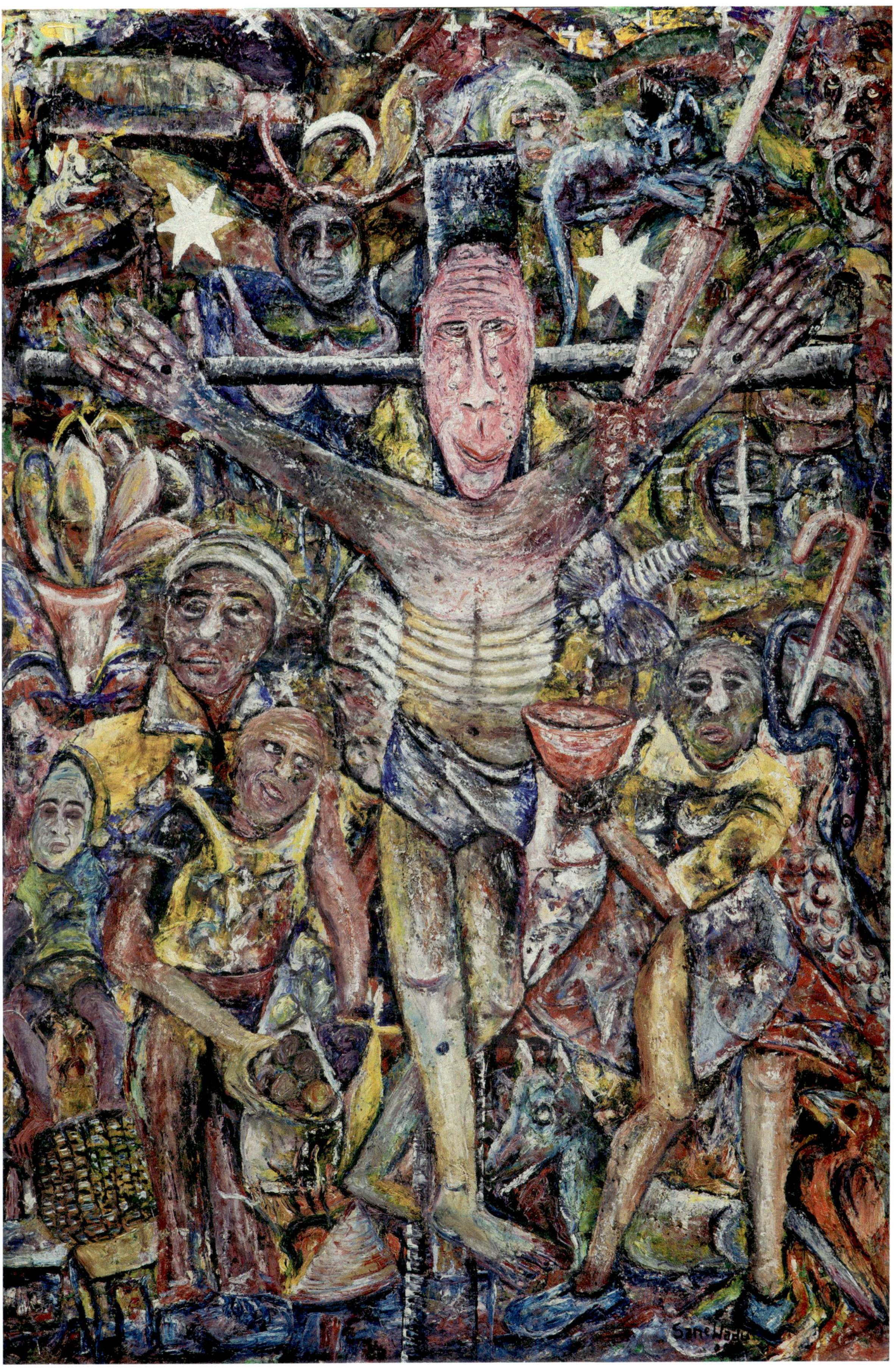
Sane Wadu

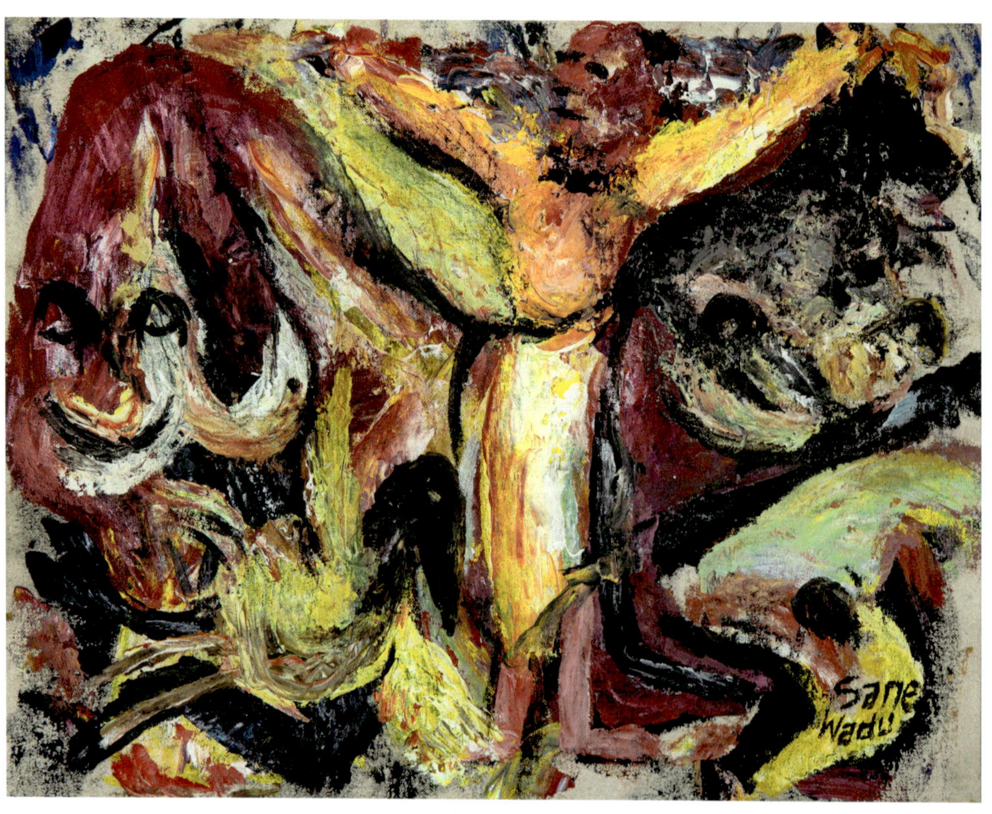

12 Afraid of Being (What One Is) *and* Unidentified Fear

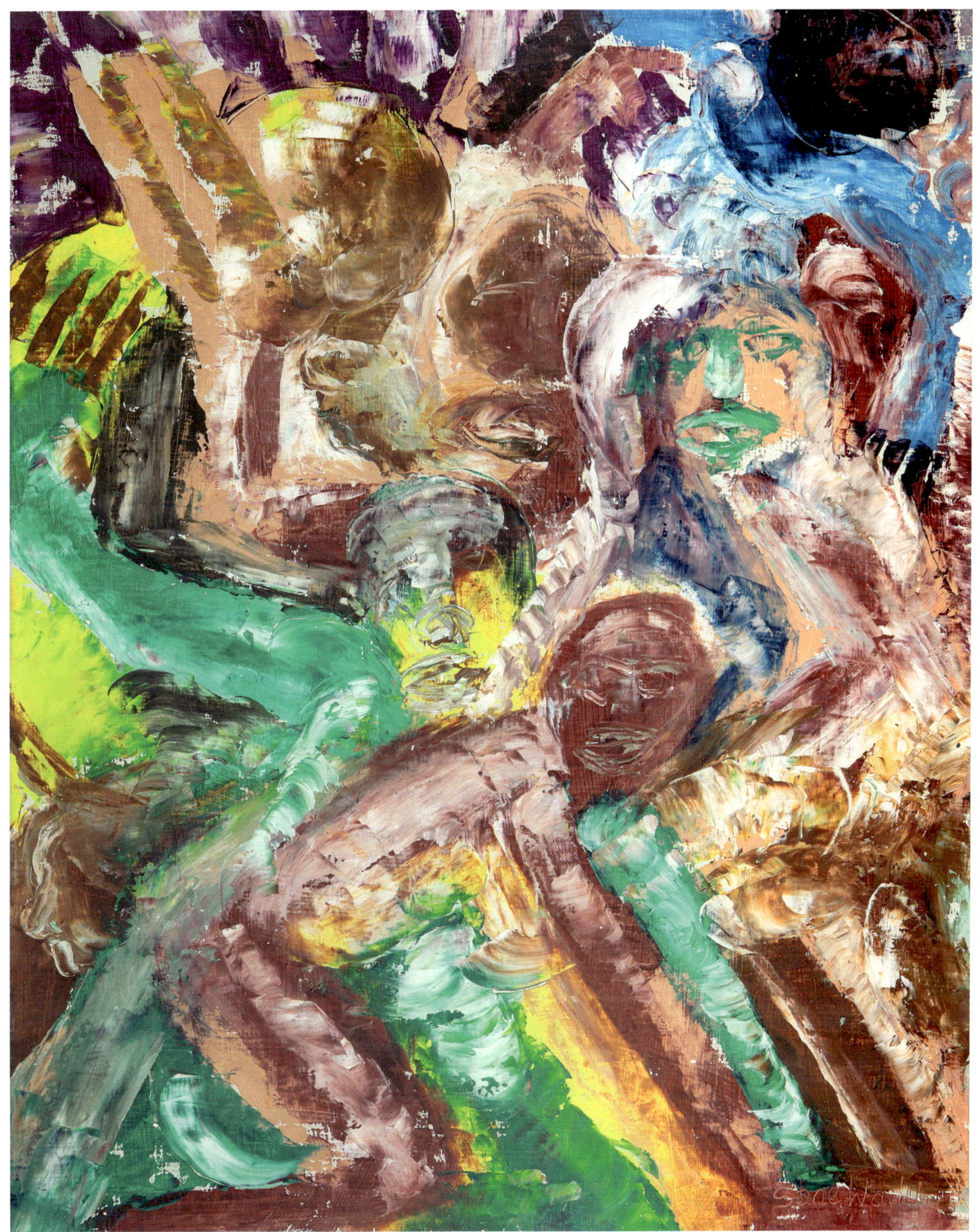
Sane Wadu

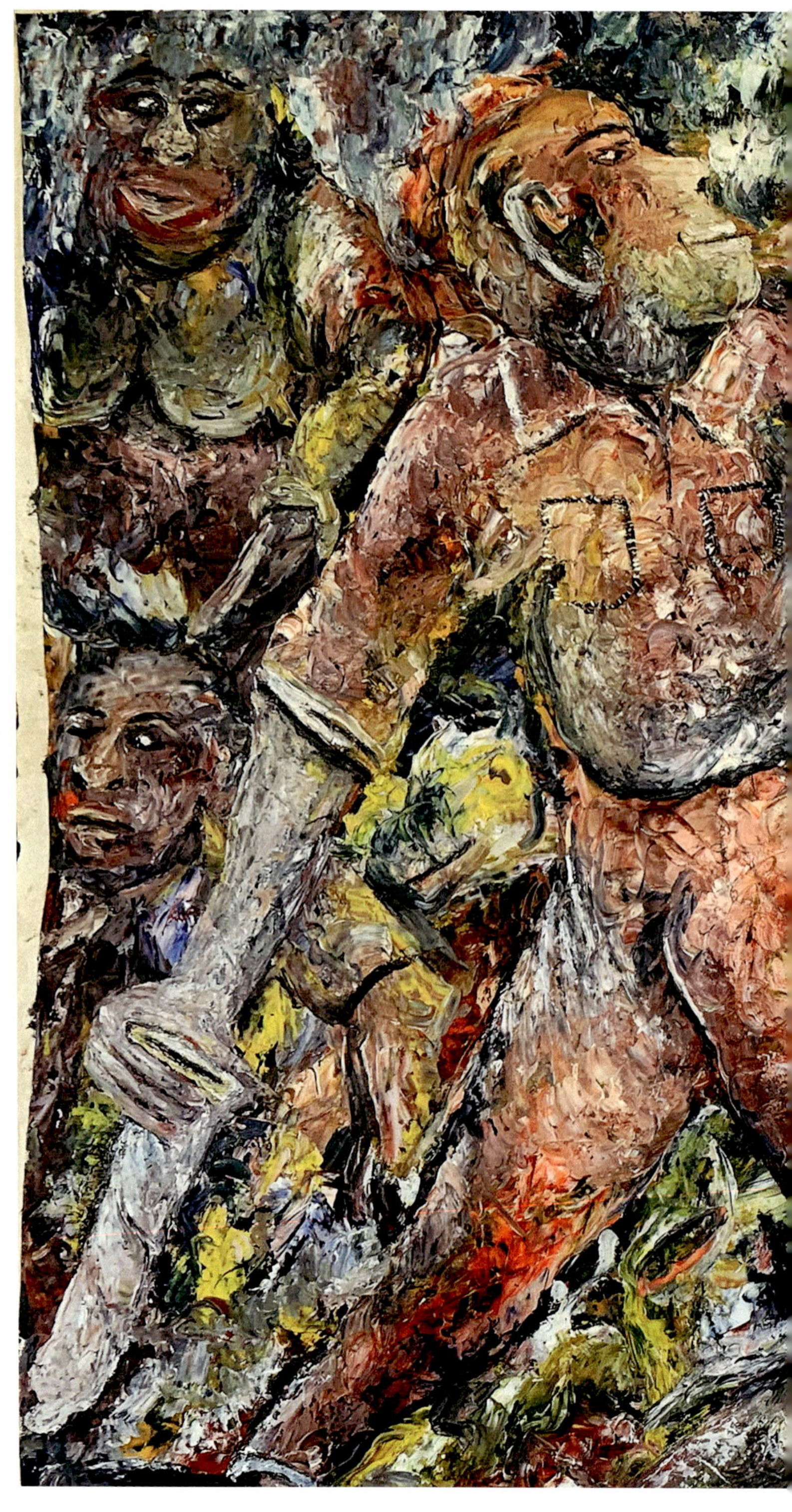

 Tit for Tat *following spread* Sitting on the Goal Post *and* Love Thy Neighbour

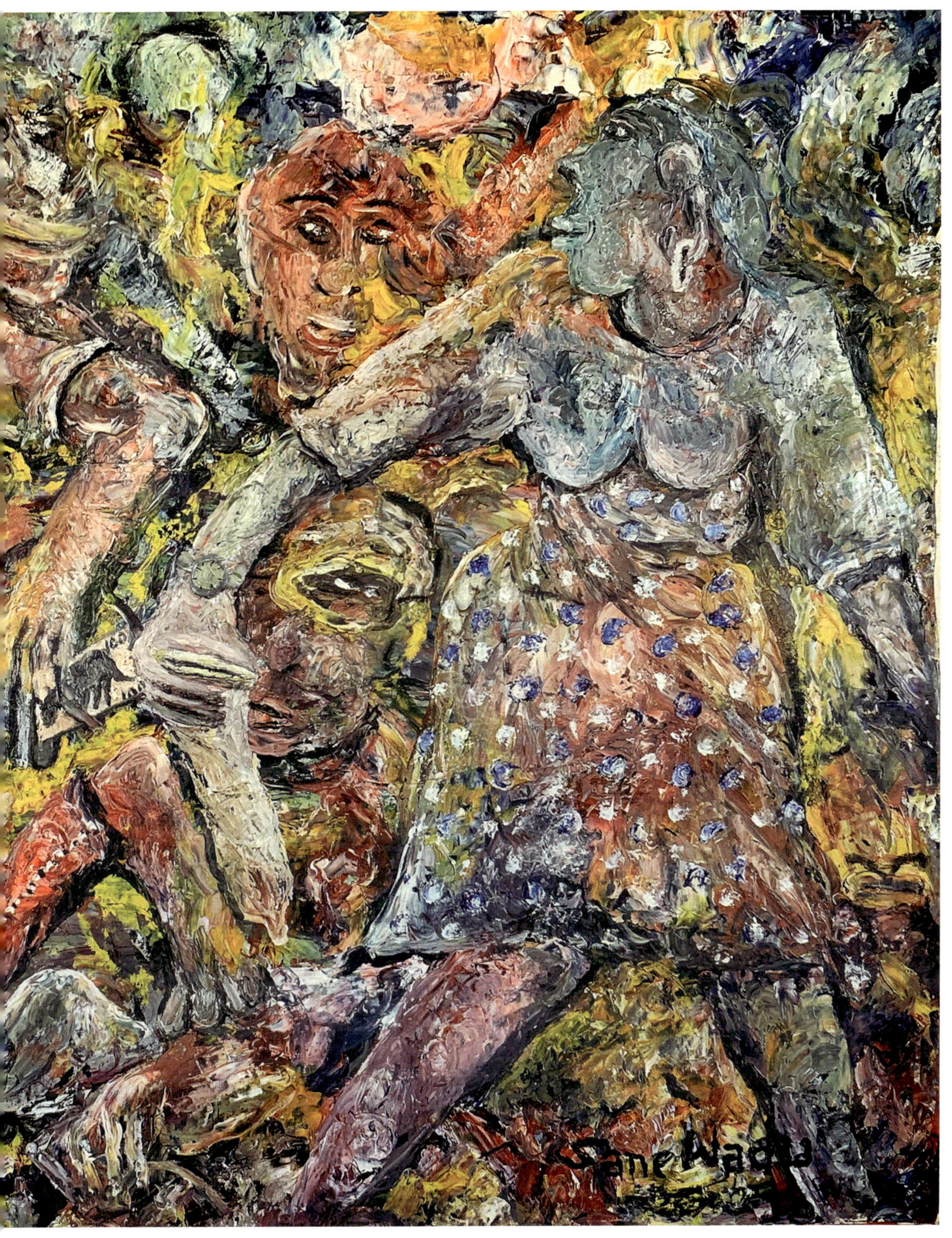
Sane Wadu

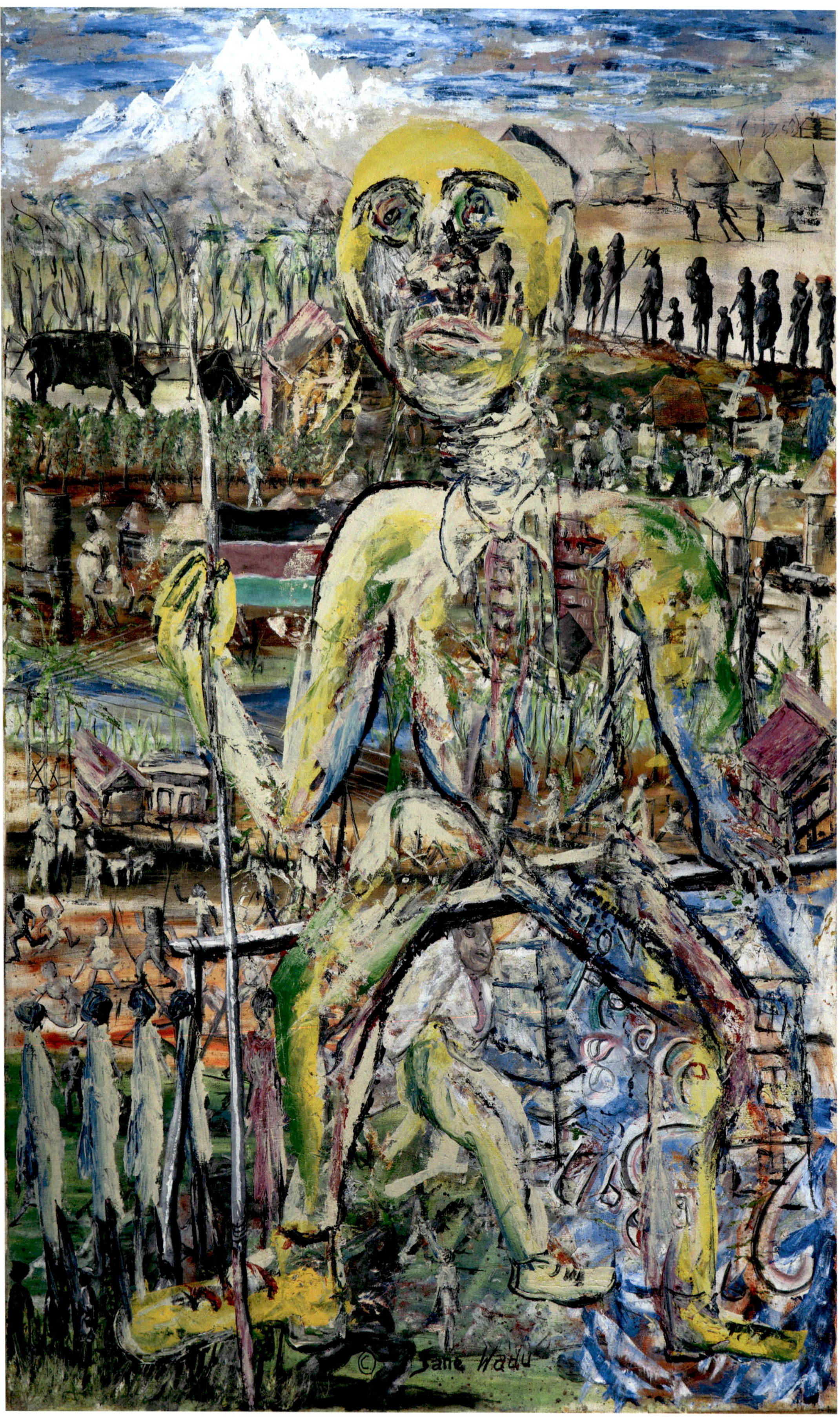
© Jane Wadu

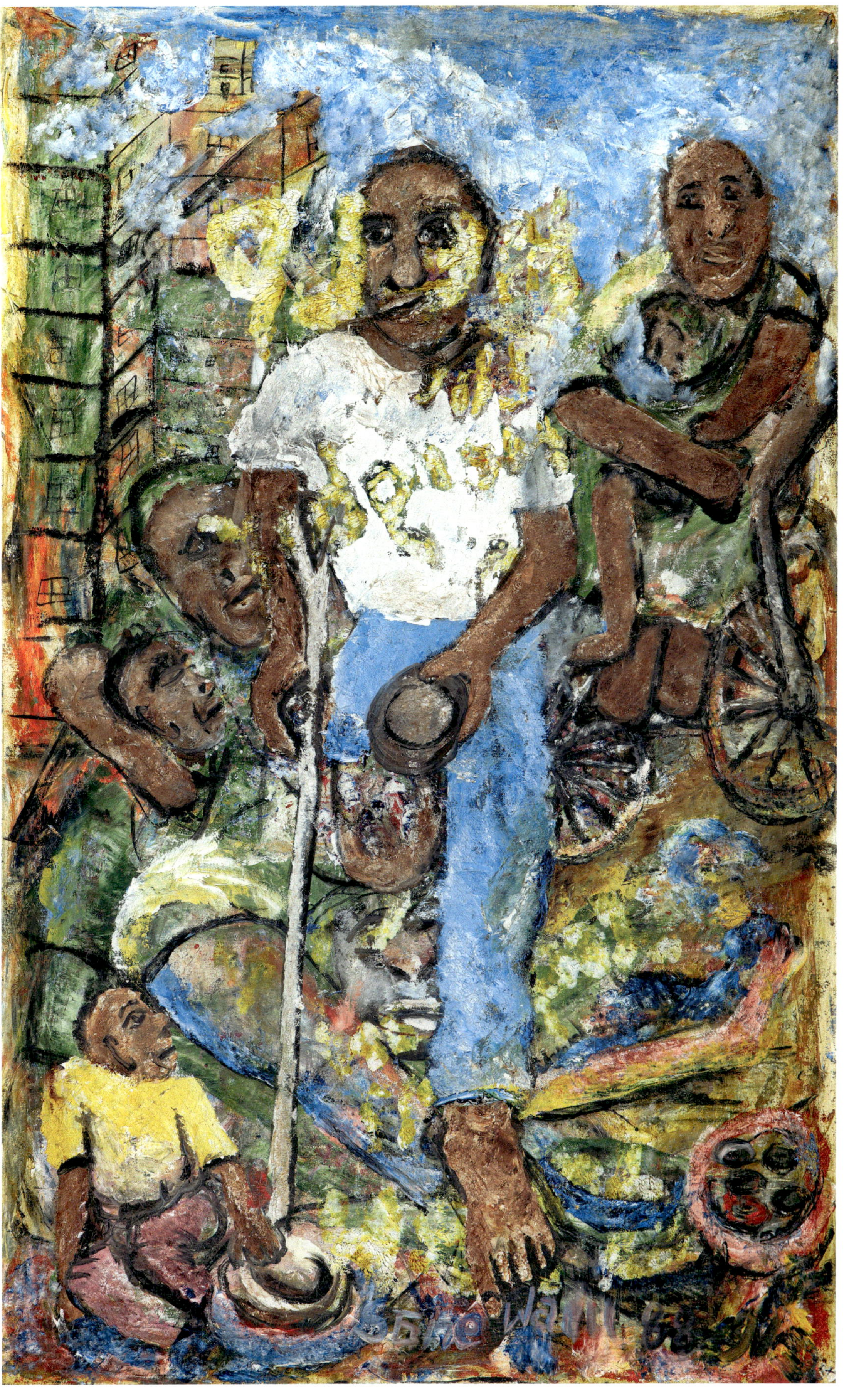

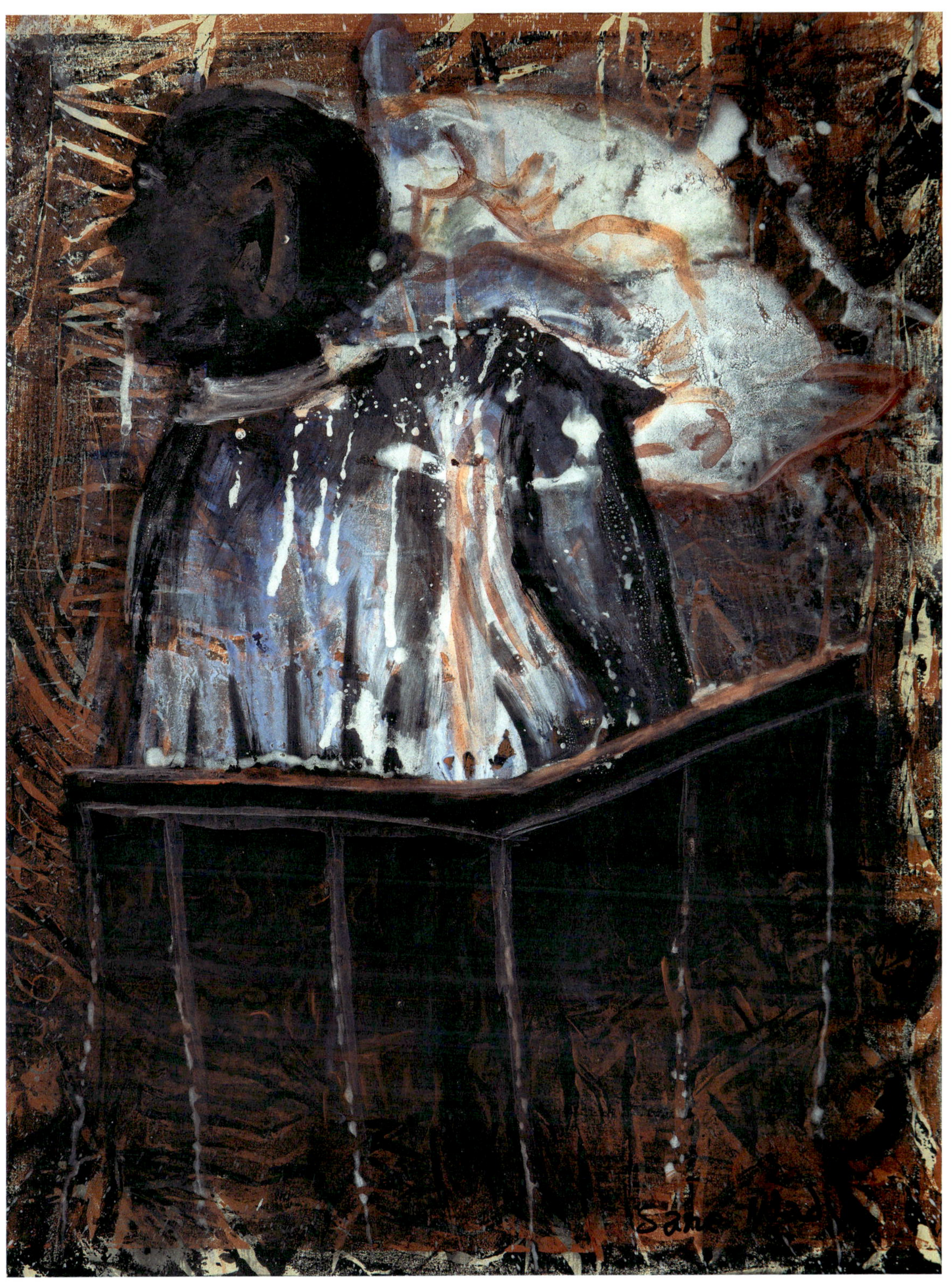

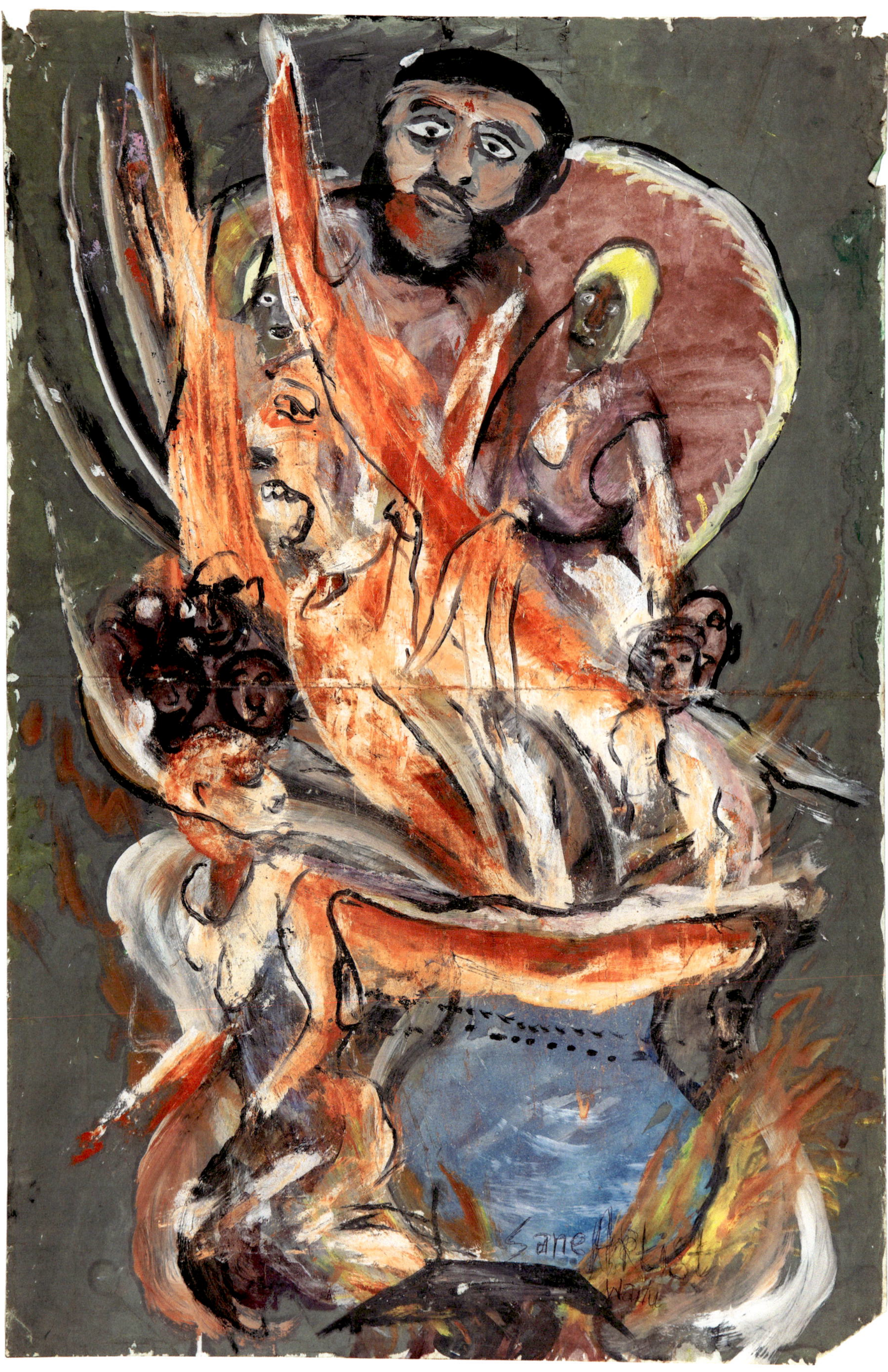

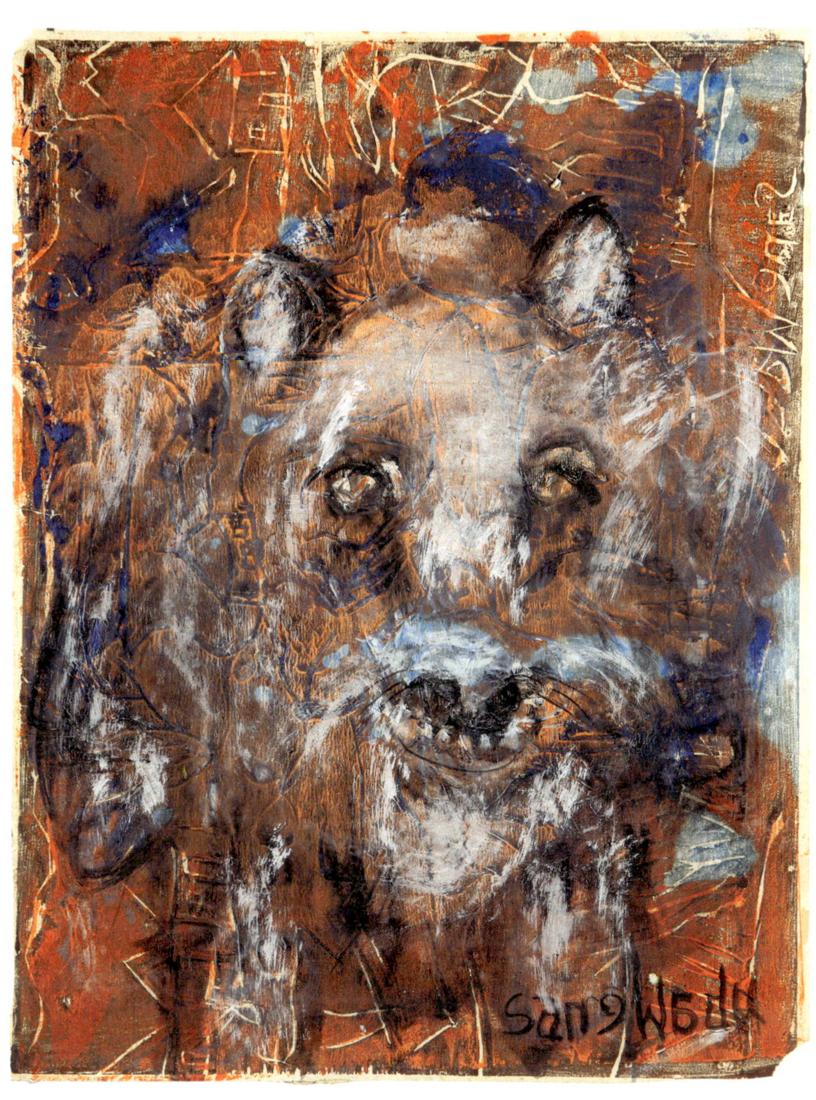

21 Hot Soup *and* King of the Jungle

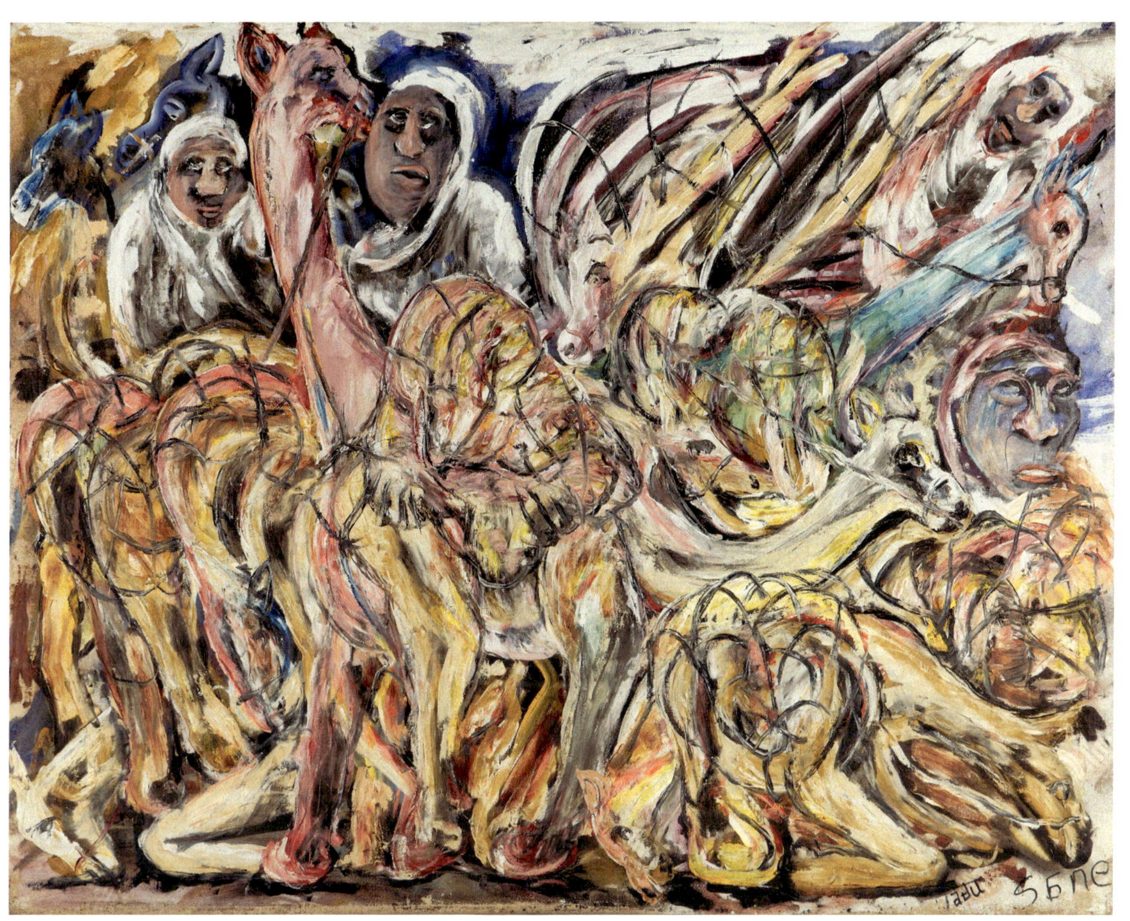

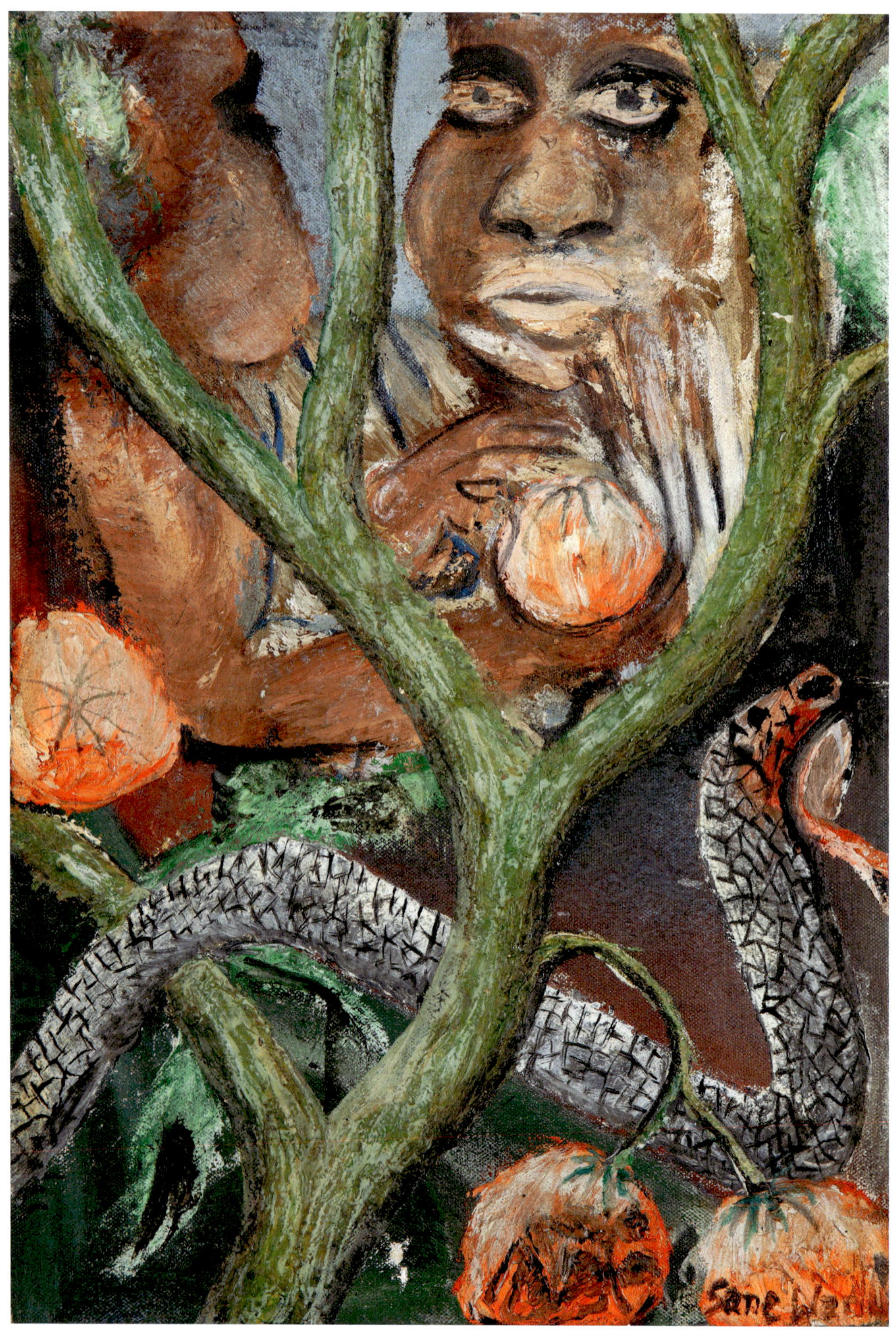

24 Adam and Eve

I HOPE SO

SANE WADU

HOPE AND DESPAIR: URI KWIIRUKIRA NDUNGITHONDEKEKA

MUKAMI KURIA

Born into peri-urban Nyathuna, in close proximity to the city, Sane Wadu's early works share an ongoing occupation with bucolic scenes of pastoral life. These works, though seemingly idyllic, are in their truest form unembellished, devoid of 'romanticism' and painted with an 'inside familiarity' of rural Kenya.[1] A triptych of experimental works depicting village scenes are emblematic of his approach to painting the ordinary from memory, nostalgia, and personal experience. The three works from 1985 are rendered in household paint on plastic sheets, demonstrating an innovativeness towards painting in conditions of scarcity, mastering the surface with ingenuity and dexterity to reflect on scenes he knows intimately. *Herds Boy* (see page 68), *From The River* (see page 69) and *Three Cows* (see page 71) reflect on gendered labour and cultural practices of animal rearing and shepherding within Kenyan society, while opening up Wadu's continued interest in the figure and dynamism of 'The Shepherd.'

Though these and other works refer to cultural practices around shepherding, the metaphor within also invokes the lens through which Wadu examines his own notions of spirituality and the arduousness of absolute faith. The Shepherd infers the canonical image of unwavering faith and spirituality proffered in Psalm 23, giving meaning to both the senses of the word pastoral and the mortal trajectory of the Christian follower. As in its biblical iteration, The [Good] Shepherd invoked in Wadu's oeuvre is specifically present as the archetypal image of Jesus Christ. The deeply evocative painting, *Bless This Our Daily Bread* (1984) (see pages 8–9), is suggestive of much of the religious iconography that unifies Kenyan visual and material culture [within domestic settings]. Iconic depictions of Christ and their ubiquity in the homes of elderly Kenyans, amongst them the first converts to Christianity, unearth nostalgia for many of Wadu's audiences, whose grandparents' and parents' homes are plastered with graphic posters of the Messiah and decorated with ceramic ornaments, inscribed with the unattributed quote: 'Christ is the head of the home, the unseen guest of every meal, the silent listener to every conversation.'[2] These ornamental displays of faith would illustrate the omnipresence of religion and prove the deep, even transcendental, pious conviction of the house's inhabitants to those who visited.

Such devotional exhibition of religious imagery recalls the impact of printmaking and prints on the spread of religion across Europe, particularly during the fifteenth and sixteenth centuries, as Reformationist movements gained prominence. Until then, religious imagery had been confined to the architecture and embellishment of churches, through works made on altarpieces, stained-glass windows, and frescoes. The spread of printmaking had the effect of democratising religious imagery by allowing the mass reproduction of affordable images, as opposed to etchings and paintings, which were limited to collections of the wealthy. These are were especially influential amongst the illiterate; the preacher Johann Geiler von Kaisersberg at Strasbourg Cathedral encouraged those in his congregation who could not read to buy one of 'those paper images on which the meeting of Mary and Elizabeth is painted [...] for a penny'[3] and instructed them to 'look at it, and think how happy they were and full of hope, and come to know that in your faith!'[4] To von Kaisersberg, acts of faith and reverence towards religious icons could inspire deep passion in moments of prayer and worship; to Wadu, his audience's collaboration in his introspective worldmaking is a truer spiritual experience.

The integral relationship between acts of seeing and listening to belief is expressed by Wadu most clearly in *Bless This Our Daily Bread*. Christ appears here meditative, eyes closed, and arms outstretched. At his feet lie fish and loaves, referencing the Feeding of the Multitude. The central figure is flanked by a disproportionate eye and ear; all-seeing and all-knowing. To believe the miracle, Wadu insinuates, you must have seen it or heard it. A miracle, derived from the Latin *mirari* meaning to wonder, necessarily elicits wonder in those who see or hear of it; the causes of miracles beyond nature or human actions. This interest in the miraculous and the sublime is present in other works such as *A Walk on Water* (see page 61), a direct reference to Christ's supernatural miracle on the Sea of Galilee when, beyond his disciples' understanding of the laws of physics, Christ calmed the storm through which he approached their boat.[5] These works are Wadu's meditations on faith as the 'strong urge to believe the impossible,'[6] as well as Wadu's innate belief in his calling to be an artist.

Despite reappropriating religious imagery as self-referential, Wadu has long rejected religion. Instead, these works are an exercise in self-reckoning and a journey of exorcising his own early religious instruction, enabling Wadu to take on a Messianic disposition that recalls his (and Christ's) status as pariah and reflects on the role of an artist in society as an oracle, a conduit for the divine, able to deliver criticism of society and salvation through his works. From the same period, *Come Closer* (1984) (see page 60) recalls Christ preaching in Judea in defiance of the Pharisees and their scrutiny, after which Christ implores the adults to let 'little children come to me, and do not hinder them, for the kingdom of God belongs to such as these'[7]. In this work, children gather around a Christlike figure, sporting Wadu's distinctive beard and sideburns and dressed in robes. Here, Wadu insinuates that his emergence as an artist and his consequent alienation from society as a madman is comparable to the distrust towards the Messiah. *Come Closer* is then a reaction to the social isolation he experienced, questioning why people evaded him while presaging the religiosity and faith in a life devoted to painting. Shepherding the children of the village to come and listen to stories, to Wadu this work encapsulates 'the spirit of feeling [being] a believer'[8], the power wielded by artists to tell stories and the mysticism and transcendental experience of viewing and reflecting on artworks.

> 'Females carry the marks, language, and nuances of their culture more than the male. Anything that is desired or despised is always placed on the female body.'[9] — Wangechi Mutu

> *Uri kwiirukira ndungithondekeka*, Kikuyu Proverb[10]
> Literal translation: If you despair, you are not cured.
> English Translation: Not to have hope is the poorest of all conditions

In 1939, G. Barra, a missionary stationed at Consolata Fathers of Nyeri, compiled *1000 Kikuyu Proverbs*. In the foreword, he wrote that the proverbs collected 'embody the maxims of natural law', apparently believing that Gikuyu knowledge was in alignment with the commandments 'written by God in the heart of all men.'[11] As such, he alleged that *uri kwiirukira ndungithondekeka* 'refer[ed] to women who go to the witch-doctors for a remedy for their sterility.'[12]

Fast-forward a few decades later, an image from 1985 – shared recently on social media by sculptor Gakunju Kaigwa[13] – is an attestation to the global eugenicist zeitgeist, to which East African artistic production was not impervious. The photograph was taken at a workshop held at Utalii Hotel by Nani Croze and Dr Eric Krystall. The pair commissioned artists to create 'posters on population and development issues'[14] which culminated in Family Planning Private Sector's (FFPS) Calendar for 1986 and a publication titled 'Artistic Visions of Family Planning'. Krystall had returned to Kenya to set up the USAID-backed FFPS at the height of the Cold War, during which the USA and USSR rushed to identify and support areas of 'socio-economic assistance'[15] in Africa, Asia, and Latin American. Kenya was no exception; in fact, the New York Times reported that the highest population growth rate was in Kenya,[16] and the World Bank sensationalised these statistics,[17] causing alarm over the fertility of Kenyan women.

Though Non-Governmental Organisations rushed to create clinics, policies, and public health education, assisting the government in implementing its population policy, these efforts were met with fierce criticism from the Catholic Church. From his pulpit, Archbishop Cardinal Maurice Otunga would denounce 'family planning activists' and government policies for their interference, later fighting a verbal battle with then Vice President Mwai Kibaki 'over the establishment of 'government sterilization camps' in rural areas.'[18] Otunga contended that contraception was contrary to Christian teachings and to Pope John Paul VI's *Human Vitae: On The Regulation of Life*. In 1996, at the height of the AIDS crisis, Otunga was once again in the newspapers, setting fire to condoms and safe-sex literature at a ceremony intended to 'highlight Church teaching on the immorality of contraception and sex outside of marriage.'[19]

Through the FFPS workshops and calendars, Kenyan artists, too, were incorporated into the ideological and theological debates and policy interventions carried out on the bodies of Kenyans gendered as women. From the 1987 Report, 'New Paths To Family Planning,' illustrated with works fabricated during the workshop, 'the artists' images and concepts were carefully pre-tested to assess their effectiveness'[20] in conveying family planning methods. Dr Krystall and FFPS employed the artworks to communicate to their audiences 'in view of the relatively high rate of illiteracy,' selecting artworks which conveyed most aptly 'the realities that fit clients' lives.'[21]

The artists pictured at the very first workshop did not include Wadu, but contemporaries of his, among them Ancent Soi, Nuwa Wamala Nnyanzi, Sukuro Etale and Jak Katarikawe, whose later works in '*The Lovers*' Series carry the legacy of these workshops. Wadu, taking part in later workshops shows that the themes of the workshop permeated the practices of the artists who took part, making work not only in response to the projects carried out by FFPS, but continuing to grapple with family planning and developmental economics in the privacy of their studios. Maternal precarity, for example, is a question Wadu returns to often, evident in his paintings from the late 90s, *A Single Mother* (see page 3) and *Begging Mother,* which ruminate on the feminised labour of caregiving, absence, and other hardships of mothering. He is wary of glorifying and idolising the fertility of mothers, evading tropes such as the one depicted by Katarikawe in *Mama Africa* (1985), which is the cover image of the FFPS Calendar and Publication. While Katarakiwe's painting affirmed the NYT's claim that the customary veneration due to women for their fertility was one of the challenges that remained 'powerful in the face of policies to curb population growth' as 'a wife's worth [would] be judged by her fertility,'[22] Wadu's *Long Legs (Things Men Do)* (2005) (see page 55) mockingly turns his audience's attention to the subsequent observation that 'to men, numerous offspring are living symbols of virility.'[23] The entirety of the work is taken up by two disembodied legs which frame the vague outline of a penis, referencing the myth that 'children come from the bones of men'[24] and that taller men are therefore more fertile.

Yet the painting *Mother Dragon* (see page 6) breaks free from the limited frames of NGO-produced artworks made by Wadu's peers and from the glorification of fertility and of the suffering of women. An unsettling work, executed in deep purple and blue hues, the painting depicts a woman with disproportionate overarching arms. From her womb emerge faces and suggestions of bodies, which appear to remain a part of her body, still. The multiplicity of the figures and the seeming inability of the mother to hold all her children are an intimate and honest depiction of hardship. Wadu's focus on the mother and the conspicuous absence of the father challenges the dogma espoused by Otunga and others in the Catholic church, on the archetypal heteronormative Christian family.

It is a deeply perceptive work that challenges the viewer to question religious teachings and biblical narratives around procreation, and societal norms around childbearing and caregiving.

Revisiting sexual politics in later works, Wadu has established himself as one of the foremost commentators on gender and societal expectations. He remains ever the provocateur, while his language shifts, turning his gaze to confront the incoherence in the ideologies espoused by institutions. In the 2014 work, *Tit for Tat* (see pages 14–15), Wadu's quick and fluid brushstrokes are suggestive of a fervour and freedom within his use of impasto. In the hazy image invoking seedy nightclubs, the viewer can make out two complete figures amidst a sea of partially rendered heads and figures. Clearest of all are the condoms in the hands of the man and the woman. In his notes, Wadu writes that this work is about 'the love game [and] safe sex.'[25] The language of safe sex, exemplary of NGO campaigns and foreign policy from the Bush-era, is seemingly inescapable, and it pervades Wadu's own register. Turning language on itself, however, the original framework is unsettled and probed by Wadu – 'for whom?' he asks. The painting probes the inequality of family planning and agency in the use of contraceptive methods. The representation of the condoms becomes a device through which Wadu questions whether an alternative is possible; 'if a man uses a male condom, the female should reciprocate and insist to have a female condom. Which is better? The choice is yours.'[26] Wadu, like the Kikuyu medicine men, proposes his own alternatives for women – not by offering remedies for infertility, but by imagining differently the sexual agency of women, as detached from decision-making by men. For a moment, his work is a tonic for societal contradictions. The artist, critical of society, diagnoses and purports to offer his own cures to that which ails Kenyan society. Through Wadu, we are hopeful.

30 December 2002. In the sun, hundreds of thousands of Kenyans gathered in Uhuru Park seem to have melted into a restless and indistinct mass. The hill beneath Afya House is covered in its entirety, spectators clinging to lampposts and dotted amongst the branches of trees. On Processional Way, those present are wearing NARC campaign posters as hats, while others wave palm branches, chanting 'we want peace!' as horseback members of the General Service Unit try to control them. They wave the branches, invoking the biblical image of Palm Sunday and Christ's entry into Jerusalem met with similar crowds shouting 'Hosanna!' and 'Blessed is he who comes in the name of the Lord!'[27]. The optimism of the crowd and the nation is most aptly captured by one man's poster which reads: 'KIBAKI IS OUR MOSES'.[28]

The scenes at Uhuru Park in 2002 speak to a focal work within the retrospective: the sweeping painting *Black Moses*, made in 1993 (see pages 56–57). As one of the larger works in Wadu's oeuvre, and the largest work in the exhibition, the artist's masterful use of scale creates a politically charged work, in which the density of the work and figuration act as a veil for Wadu's subtle criticism of leadership in Kenya. The faceless mass of countless figures is dwarfed by the central figure in the painting, the apparent leader and Godhead whose identity, though concealed, bears a likeness to then-President Moi. They prostrate on their knees in undeniable distress and despair, some with their hands raised and others with their faces turned away from their ruler.

Wadu appropriates and retells the biblical allegory of Moses leading the Israelites out of Egypt into Canaan, but interrupts the characterisation of Moses as a saviour. Instead, Wadu's *Black Moses*, becomes a covert device for the artist to examine the relationship between the ruler and the ruled, at a time when political and artistic repression were rife in Kenya. In Wadu's words, the absence of the rule of law creates the necessary lacuna for the leader to 'use force to oppress and suppress their citizens'[29] – the ruler in *Black Moses* is protected by gun-wielding figures immediately beneath him. Languishing under the weight of the leader, the citizens are overwhelmed by oppressive leadership. Unable to protest injustice, 'they [are] crying to God to save their souls from much oppression'[30]. The leader meant to emancipate them is now usurped by religion which stands as their true form of salvation.

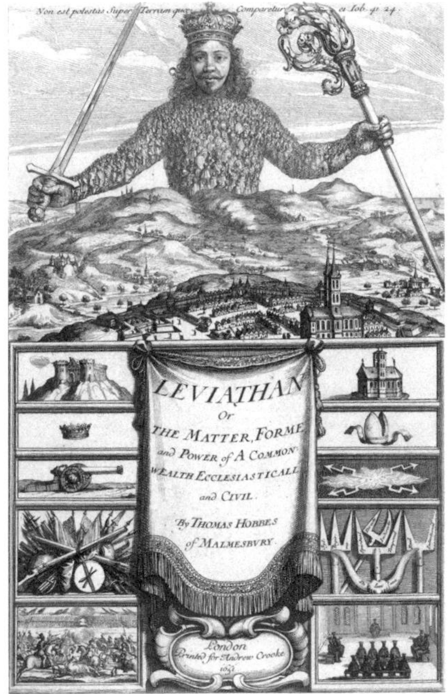

Here, Wadu questions the dynamic between leaders and their followers. The leader is distinguishable from his followers, and yet is constituted of and derives his legitimacy from them. Gaining authority from the people, this painting and the figure of the ruler recall the Hobbesian 'body politic' and 'artificial man'.[31] Within the Hobbesian social contract, the people cede their freedom to 'destroy one another', in exchange for security and peace guaranteed by the 'Sovereign', their absolute representative.[32] In the body politic, 'a multitude of men are

33 Frontispiece of Thomas Hobbes' *Leviathan*, by Abraham Bosse, 1651

made one person when they are by one man, or one person represented'[33] and their consent to government is total and indivisible. Visually, this is suitably captured in the Frontispiece of Leviathan, illustrated by Abraham Bosse. The ruler's body and arms are constituted of hundreds of people, turned towards him in allegiance, the ruler rising above the landscape and armed with a sword and crosier, symbols of earthly and divine authority.

The centrality of monotheistic faith to politics, predominantly postcolonial Christianity, has remained constant within the Kenyan political landscape and within Wadu's practice. Emancipatory rhetoric, dreams and narratives of hope are peddled to Kenyans each election cycle by politicians, enabled and empowered by powerful religious men and women. The figure of the politician and the religious leader become transposable; Sunday morning church services become stages for impassioned political rallies, substantial tithes are given to sanitise those accused of corruption and politicians purport to be anointed with a God-given right to lead. From their podiums or pulpits, religious and political leaders reconfigure space and command audiences seeking redemption, salvation, and escape, in truth delivering empty promises and false virtue. Wadu recounts first moving to Naivasha, where a preacher in the town was the image of perfect devotion. From his compound throughout the night, the neighbourhood would hear him in impassioned prayer. Only later did Wadu discover that the preacher would climb a tree, mount a megaphone and play a cassette recording of him praying, while he returned to the comfort of his bed.

A Pope (see page 54) and *This Way to Mecca,* two paintings from the 1990s, further tease out the untrustworthiness of religious leaders, with Wadu confusing the works for one another in his artist notes and inadvertently merging them into an interchangeable narrative perspective. *A Pope* – once again depicted as Wadu, as he did with Christ – recalls the visit of Pope John Paul II to Nairobi and 'promises the people which way is heaven'[34]. The structure and figuration of the Head of the Catholic Church, depicted with outstretched hands, suggest that the painting is a portal to Paradise, grounded in canvas and inviting its audience to travel through the work in pursuit of deliverance. The suggestion of promises and hopefulness are consistent within Wadu's work, yet the culmination of these hopes is hope unfulfilled. In this painting Wadu asks of the Pope, 'is he our hope to Canaan?'[35] Yet in a recent conversation with Wadu, further probing of the words written on the back surface of a similar painting alleged to be *A Pope* reveals that its true title is entirely different. '*This Way to Mecca*' the actual title of the work, is said to be a depiction of Ayatollah Khomeini and his followers on a boat. Inadvertently, then, the Biblical and Qur'anic holy lands meet in Wadu's mistaken confusion over the two paintings and their titles, with the artist offering the delicious provocation and suggestion that the Pope and the Ayatollah themselves may lead their followers down unknown paths in the name of salvation, and that this pedestalization of religious figures and lack of transparency are just as questionable as the political demands of the nation-state. If the destination of monotheistic religions is the afterlife – Jannah or Heaven – Wadu suggests that an individual journey of critical faith offers more clarity. His deep scepticism of religious and political leaders is a warning to viewers of his paintings: false prophets and false politicians will not save you.

His careful consideration of religion and politics has been a decades-long practice of critical self-retrospection, finding a way to 'consider these things' himself, and he encourages his audiences to do the same. In the void left by unfulfilled promises, hollowness remains, and yet from a fertile absence, Wadu reminds us that another way is possible and there could always be a future imagined differently. Seek your own truths and sanity; reimagine the world anew; find hope within.

1 Author unattributed, 'Painter, Poet and Survivor', The Weekly Review, November 06, 1987.
2 Joanna Reiling Lindell, 'The Religious Print,' *The Thrivent Collection of Religious Art,* www.thriventcollection.com/learn/the-religious-print.html.
3 Lindell, 'The Religious Print.'
4 Lindell, 'The Religious Print.'
5 Matthew 14:22–34; Mark 6:45–53; John 6:15–21, New International Version.
6 Sane Wadu, Artist Notes, Undated.
7 Matthew 19: 4, New International Version.
8 Sane Wadu, Artist Notes, Undated.
9 Merrily Kerr, 'Extreme Makeovers,' *Art on Paper 8*, no.6 (2004): 28.
10 G. Barra, *1000 Kikuyu Proverbs*: *With Tranaslations and English Equivalents* (Nairobi: Macmillan, 1939), 124.
11 Barra, *1000 Kikuyu Proverbs,* 124.
12 Barra, *1000 Kikuyu Proverbs,* 124.
13 Gakunju Kaigwa, 'Blast from the past', Facebook, September 30, 2017, www.facebook.com/story.php?story_fbid=pfbid02Q8uXFCEHjPgP559JqbLEPYJYPudbCBqd5T46n84cr7×HUygVvEY-byiATc9XL7RTGl&id=625232241
14 The Family Planning Private Sector Programme of Kenya, 'New Paths to Family Planning,' November 1987, 9.
15 Eric Krystall, *Swimming Through Life: The Abiding Optimism of an African Development Worker*, (Nairobi: E. Krystall, 2012), 354.
16 Sheila Rule, 'African Rift: Birth Control vs Tradition', *New York Times*, August 11, 1985.
17 'Kenyan population growth has risen steadily from an annual rate of 2.5 percent in 1948 to around 3.8 percent in the 1980s. These trends derive from an increase in the total fertility rate (TFR) from 6 to almost 8 children over this period.' – World Bank Discussion Paper 107, 'Kenya at the Demographic Turning Point', November 30, 1991, x
18 Charles Mitchell, 'On Sundays, Nairobi's 'Holy Corner' rocks to the beat,' *United Press International*, August 08, 1985.
19 Author unattributed, 'Kenyan Cardinal Burns Condoms, Safe Sex Literature,' *Catholic World News*, September 03, 1996.
20 The Family Planning Private Sector Programme of Kenya, 'New Paths to Family Planning,' 9.
21 'New Paths to Family Planning,' 9.
22 Sheila Rule, 'African Rift: Birth Control vs Tradition,' *New York Times*, August 11, 1985.
23 Rule, 'African Rift'.
24 Sane Wadu, Artist Notes, Undated.
25 Sane Wadu, Artist Notes, Undated.
26 Sane Wadu, Artist Notes, Undated.
27 Matthew 21: 9, New International Version.
28 Michaela Wrong, *It's Our Turn to Eat* (New York City, Harper Perennial, 2009), 4.
29 Sane Wadu, Artist Notes, Undated.
30 Sane Wadu, Artist Notes, Undated.
31 Thomas Hobbes, *Leviathan* (Baltimore: Penguin Books, 1968 [1651]), 7.
32 Hobbes, *Leviathan*, 78.
33 Hobbes, *Leviathan*, 101.
34 Sane Wadu, Artist Notes, Undated.
35 Sane Wadu, Artist Notes, Undated.

VEER AND FLOW

SANE WADU IN CONVERSATION WITH ROSIE OLANG' ODHIAMBO

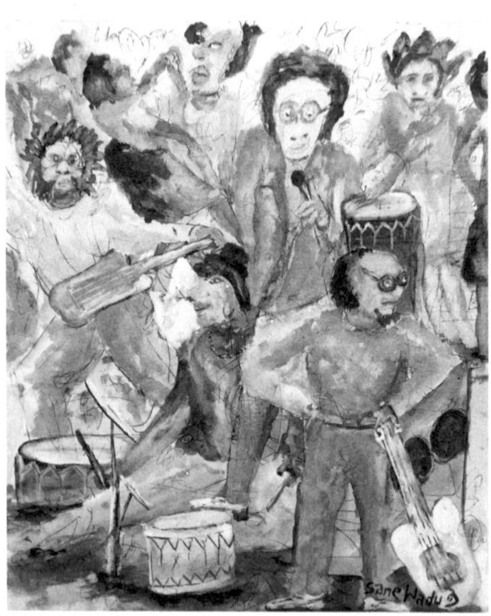

ROSIE OLANG' ODHIAMBO *Sane, you often say that you were born an artist, could we start here, tell us more?*

SANE WADU I honestly don't think there was anything else I could do. When I began painting, my parents and local community could not understand how I left a well-paying job, by the standard of those days, as a trained teacher and later a court clerk, for a field which was very uncertain, nobody could see any sense in this new direction. But for me it's about what I want to tell the world, how I want to express myself, and how I want to be understood. Initially I thought I would try my hand in music, but this did not go well. I sought out people around me who had musical instruments because I didn't have the equipment.

ROO *So there were a lot of musicians when you started out?*

SW Yes, the one-man guitar was very popular... And as much as I focussed my mind on any future prospects, it was not forthcoming in music.

ROO *This makes me think of that painting,* Sane and the Band

SW That was much later actually, but maybe references that time subconsciously. After realising the music wasn't going anywhere, I turned to theatre. With a few of my former students we organised ourselves into a successful drama club based at YMCA Ngecha, and this allowed us to pick up a few shillings to offset our daily needs. I acted twice at what was then called the Voice of Kenya (VoK), and in the community, we performed for kids in schools and in other public places for mixed audiences. While our performances were well received, you also need to think of your daily bread, and if you can't find sustenance in one

Sane and the Band, (2003) Watercolour on paper

part you try another. Unfortunately that Ngecha YMCA was also mismanaged so programmes that were run there stopped. At the time I was also writing praise and prose but that too was not moving.

ROO *On that question of getting stuck, and also that question of survival, sustaining the material conditions which enable other things, could you tell us more about that journey, that hope?*

SW When you perceive yourself in the future will you have made it? You either get stuck or go through. You have to insist, and also be patient. When you see one path isn't going as planned, you make a turn to see if you will flow; if not, you veer again. Finally, I turned to drawing. I found the language in which I was most easily understood, and it was visual art.

ROO *And going back a little, what was it like growing up in pre-independence Kenya?*

SW in those days before independence, people were put in villages, you know, and this is why we have the Ngecha Village, Nyathuna village, etc...

ROO *Technically those were reservations?*

SW Yes, indigenous African communities were relocated to live there by white settlers who would allocate families a plot in a village and a farm far away. The residents were not allowed to build in the farms further away. This way they were able to control people's movements.

But slowly people started to realise their freedoms. For example, my father was about the third or fourth person to reject that law and build on his farm. We took apart our home in the village and settled there.

ROO *Tell me more about those early years?*

SW There were 12 of us, twelve siblings and I was the second born. We were an entire football team plus a reserve.

ROO *And this was in Nyathuna?*

SW Yes, Nyathuna in about 1965, 1966. I remember I was in standard two that's where I understood how to write the word 'thuruari.' My parents were farmers, survivors really. At present, I have three kids and I think about how difficult it must have been to provide for 12 children, but they succeeded. This was also from the mindset that every child has been planned for by God.

[*In Kikuyu 'thuruari' means pants or underwear*]

ROO *And do you believe that?*

SW Even God is not foolish. I don't know. But it's also that same mindset that you could be giving birth to a ruler, a leader, you know. I sometimes think that if I stayed in Nyathuna I would be a District Officer, a few of my family members were chiefs and I would have pushed myself further to be a District Officer.

ROO *But you didn't stay in Nyathuna?*

SW Yes.

ROO *When was that first transition?*

SW When I went to Kirangari High School.

ROO *Is that where you began to draw or you were yet to?*

SW That was where I wore my first shoes. We were given uniforms and books by the school. But also, as a Form 1 I was really bullied by the seniors. I paid my dues

ROO *And was there still a very strong connection between formal education at the time and missionary and church activities?*

SW We were not forced. But because we were children, we were introduced to the Christian religious teachings. I do think that children need that foundation, because they acquire some kind of fear. But as you begin to mature, and consider these things for yourself, and looking around, you start to find there is no more truth, the way you've been made to see things.

ROO *And for you when did you arrive at that?*

SW When I was still very young. I guess we were rebels. In primary school, we would go around a mugumo tree seven times, and we could do that without any fear. Some other children would go four times and stop, but as for me, I would even go up to ten times. At the same time there were very staunch Christians, and we didn't understand why. If you've heard the song Itikia Ngai, which in Kikuyu language means Believe in God, but we understood it as chair of God, you see that difference?

[*There is a Kikuyu traditional belief that if one goes around a Mugumo tree 7 times, their gender would change*]

ROO *Ah, so it sounds both like 'Chair of God' and 'Belief in God?'*

SW Yes, and we didn't understand what the fuss was all about? This also reminds me, when we first moved to Naivasha, there used to be a preacher who in the nighttime, would climb a tree in an old man's compound and attach a cassette player to a megaphone, such that the people in the neighbourhood would think he is a very devoted Christian, praying at us all night, and yet he was asleep.

ROO *And when did you move to Naivasha?*

SW In 1990

ROO *And this was from Ngecha?*

SW No, we left Ngecha in 89' and lived in Rongai briefly before Naivasha.

ROO *And how was that transition, from Ngecha, to Rongai, and then to Naivasha?*

SW Well it's just life. I was a young man with a little money.

ROO *I'm curious about how the Ngecha Artist Association came to be; what was it like day to day?*

SW By this time, I was already learning as an artist. When we were coming out in '85, '86, not many people recognised us as artists, we were strangers in the community. Many people would look at us as though we were mad. There was music, there was theatre, there was writing, all that did not move, but now, I was making a name for myself as a painter, and others were, too.

So in the association, we began with Wanyu Brush, who also insisted on being an artist, we had Eunice, Muhandi, Sebastian Kiarie and the late King Dodge. And so our minds came together to help the larger community through the artist association, which was supported by Ruth Schaffner of Gallery Watatu. And I think it's the mentality that when you open a business, and it succeeds, everyone tries the business as well, but eventually a few people joined and soon began to phase themselves out. They began to understand that art was not magic.

ROO *So people dropped off?*

SW Yes, many. But if you don't have the passion for it, sooner than later you get tired. I was able to make a name for myself as an artist, as a painter. So we hosted workshops for two or three years, and would try to mentor aspiring artists, and then it became like our politicians, you know? You don't want to be led, you want to lead, so inevitably, that 'korogakoroga' got into the mix. And Eunice and I felt we couldn't continue butting heads with people, and it wasn't necessary for all the artist minds to be in Nairobi anyway, so we decided to move to another side and left it to them. When we settled in Naivasha we started workshops with street families. They were coming on Saturdays. We had that running for two years. We also started working with Rob Burnett, who supported the youth program until 2007 when the country experienced post-election violence.

ROO *I'm curious about your influences as an artist, what moves you?*

SW Those days, I told you as children, we had been planted with some fears about religion, so for me it was first to go back to religion, and you find that in most of my works. But that was not my way because I'm not a preacher. As soon as you let it out, you express yourself and move away. It feels like you're swimming, you just leave it behind.

ROO *Like now you've solved it; you've resolved what needed to happen there. Can we talk about a few of your works from that time, like* Self-portrait, *1985 (see page 58).*

SW This is from an even earlier time.

ROO *Ha, okay, maybe tell us more about the self-referential ways you show up in the work*

SW Whether it's my early work or more recent work, it's done by the same person, the same soul, so not much would change. Like *A Walk on Water* (see page 61) – that one that I sold was the third of its kind. The first was a test. I painted on both sides of the manila sheet. And I believed I could walk on water, I had that conscious, that I could really, so I depicted myself walking on water. I painted another really lovely one, *Mother Fate*. It was sold a long time ago, I don't know who owns it. It was another one in the same series of walking on water.

ROO *What then is being an artist if you could walk on water?*

SW Yes, it's the belief, because my mind is expressing itself, exactly the way I want it. Suppose I'm walking on water. Angela Muritu, the Assistant curator on the exhibition, once asked if anybody's ever mentioned that I paint myself looking a bit like Jesus. I supposed some people will have different perceptions. Some will say this is the devil, you know some people have that mentality?

ROO *Maybe we can also talk a little about* Bless this Our Daily Bread *(see pages 8–9)?*

SW This painting is a push-back on my previous conditioning. It was done in the same period of time. We were told there were five loaves and two fish, and a large congregation waiting to be fed, and here he is praying for the Bread. And the big ear, and the big eye, you can see and you can hear. And it's a miracle, you have to witness the miracle.

ROO *And then there is* Picking Tea *(see page 1)...*

SW Yes, it's the experience in the tea farms.

ROO *And did you work in the tea farms?*

SW Of course, we had to. We used to go to those farms to work, hiding from family. So the old man only knew you were from work when you bought something new. When I told him I wanted this or that, he would say it was only possible when he gets some money. But sometimes that wait was long. He was very much against us working, because he felt that he was the one to provide, and his reputation in the village would be tainted.

ROO *So you would sneak out to go to work?*

SW Yes, and he would later see me with the things I had asked him for, but he would never really say anything. At the point I was painting this, money was coming in steadily, Gallery Watatu under Ruth Schaffner's leadership was supporting me both technically and monetarily, and my work was being exhibited and promoted in the gallery.

ROO *Now that we're talking about this lineage of painting, from the early ones to more recent ones, I'm curious to know if there was ever a time you felt a monumental shift?*

SW The main difference was a shift in scale; moving from small, to bigger and even bigger and more ambitious, you know. It was easier to attack the canvas when it was smaller. But later you have to realise the viability of working larger is limited too, because not everyone will be buying a large painting.

ROO *And how did that feel, working larger?*

SW I had room to express myself more... there is more space

ROO *A bigger problem to solve*

SW Yes, but I had to find a balance. Working both big and small.

ROO *I'm curious about how your other travels influenced your work*

SW A long time ago I was in New York in 1989, just for a show, for about a month. I also travelled for a few Triangle workshops, in 1994 I travelled to Mbile, Zambia for two weeks, in New York again in 1998 at the World Trade Centre, and in 2001 to Trinidad and Tobago for the Big River workshop where I stayed a little longer for a residency. In 2000, I also did some interstate exhibition travels in the US; I was in Georgia, Washington DC and Massachusetts. But I can't say that the travelling influenced my work significantly really, maybe if I stayed longer it could have influenced the work more.

ROO *And with these experiences, even if it they didn't show up in the work, what did a change of place translate to, if anything*

SW My work quite often could not fit in certain spaces. It looked different, you know, and whoever loved it is a real art lover; because it was hard to define; is it fine art, is it abstract, you know. It doesn't easily fit into their categories. I also felt that if you stay longer, you get wholly influenced; you end up taking on the whole thing. Like I have a friend who stayed there painting, but he had to do other jobs, you know? So that you survive, but also, so that you forget your work, unless you know what you're doing so that you intermarry your work with whatever is there – the environment – so that you remain yourself

ROO *It would be important to find that balance.*

SW And really, that is very possible because you cannot survive as an artist who is introducing himself there, so you're either a part of that if you're staying longer and joining the system, or you're just left out. So, you've got to get in the system and assimilate.

ROO *Could we talk about your poems a little bit?*

SW Yes, What is in the poems has gone through the paintings, has been part of the painting, stemming sometimes from a chapter or maybe a few words of it, but now in a different medium. That's why you heard me say, in most of my writing, the critique is that I have to develop a character, you know, create the scene, but that shows up in the painting. It is about the feeling I had, and trying to expand it into words. But I have been unsuccessful in publishing, so I despaired but still kept it. Like my fiction has rested quietly on my computer for a long-time, until recently, when I return to it when I want new ideas to paint, I try to go back and see what I was writing.

ROO *That's interesting because you can constantly go back and harvest from it.*

SW Yes, it changes form from writing to painting.

ROO *Sane, how do you get to the point at which you know a painting is finished, and it's time to sign it?*

SW Yes, because there's nothing more to add. I'm working on a painting which is stuck and I've not yet signed because I've not yet decided if it's there, you know, I don't know where it is going. When it comes to that, sometimes I turn it side to side and upside-down. Until later, I don't know. So it is to see it and say now that thing is finished. In any painting I'm telling a story, as we are moving forward.

List of works

Picking Tea, 1985
Gouache on paper
64.8 × 48.54 cm
(25 ½ × 19 ⅛ inches)
Fairholme Collection

Lying in Trees, 1987
Gouache on Paper
55.9 × 40.3 cm
(22 × 15 ⅞ inches)
Fairholme Collection

A Single Mother, 1996
Oil on canvas
58.4 × 47.5 cm
(23 × 18 ¾ inches)

Broken Calabash, 1984
Oil on canvas
66.5 × 88.9 cm
(26 ⅛ × 35 inches)

Mother Dragon, 1988
Watercolour on paper
51 × 75.8 cm
(20 ⅛ × 29 ⅞ inches)

Hopeless Future, 1985
Oil on canvas
63.5 × 78.9 cm
(25 × 31 ⅛ inches)

Bless This Our Daily Bread, 1984
Watercolour on paper
46.99 × 69.85 cm
(18 ½ × 27 ½ inches)

Shall We Crucify him, 2000
Oil on canvas
185 × 123.8 cm
(72 ⅞ × 48 ¾ inches)

Afraid of Being (What One Is), 1988
Oil on paper
40.6 × 54 cm
(16 × 21 ¼ inches)

Unidentified Fear, 1989
Oil on canvas
50.6 × 39.6 cm
(19 ⅞ × 15 ⅝ inches)

Tit For Tat, 2014
Oil on canvas
81.3 × 111.8 cm
(32 × 44 inches)

Sitting on the Goal Post, 2001
Mixed media on canvas
131.3 × 81.5 cm
(51 ¾ × 32 ⅛ inches)
Fairholme Collection

Love Thy Neighbour, 1988
Oil on canvas
133.8 × 83.7 cm
(52 ⅝ × 33 inches)

Blessed, 1990
Mixed media on paper
51.5 × 38.9 cm
(20 ¼ × 15 ⅜ inches)

Hot Soup, 1987
Watercolour on paper
75.7 × 51 cm
(29 ¾ × 20 ⅛ inches)

King of the Jungle, 1989
Mixed print on paper
50.5 × 40 cm
(19 ⅞ × 15 ¾ inches)

Msafiri, 2000
Oil on canvas
121 × 157 cm
(47 ⅝ × 61 ¾ inches)

Adam and Eve, 1990
Oil on canvas
40.1 × 27.8 cm
(15 ¾ × 11 inches)
Fairholme Collection

Antelope, 1987
Oil on paper
50.45 × 39.3 cm
(19 ⅞ × 15 ½ inches)

Ants Bear, 1997
Mixed media on canvas
53 × 75.8 cm
(20 ⅞ × 29 ⅞ inches)

Night Shift, 2000
Oil on canvas
121.7 × 111.2 cm
(47 ⅞ × 43 ¾ inches)

Life Conspiracy, 2019
Oil on canvas
65.8 × 50.1 cm
(25 ⅞ × 19 ¾ inches)

A Pope, 1999
Oil on canvas
51.8 × 61.9 cm
(20 ⅜ × 24 ⅜ inches)

Long Legs (Things Men Do), 2005
Mixed media on paper
75.9 × 51 cm
(29 ⅞ × 20 ⅛ inches)

Black Moses, 1993
Oil on canvas
136.1 × 193.4 cm
(53 ⅝ × 76 ⅛ inches)

Self Portrait, 1985
Mixed media on paper
28.8 × 24.4 cm
(11 ⅜ × 9 ⅝ inches)

Shepherd, 1985
Watercolour on paper
24.4 × 28.8 cm
(9 ⅝ × 11 ⅜ inches)

Come Closer, 1984
Watercolour on paper,
51 × 75.7 cm
(20 ⅛ × 29 ¾ inches)

A Walk on Water, 1984
Watercolour on paper
50.4 × 76.4 cm
(19 ⅞ × 30 ⅛ inches)

Beast of Burden, 1998
Woodcut print on paper
52 × 62.6 cm
(20 ½ × 24 ⅝ inches)

My House Gallery, 1989
Watercolour on paper
50.9 × 75.7 cm
(20 × 29 ¾ inches)

Eunice, 1989
Watercolour on Paper
48 × 72 cm
(18 ⅞ × 28 ⅜ inches)
Fairholme Collection

Carpenter, 1989
Watercolour on paper
38 × 50.4 cm
(15 × 19 ⅞ inches)

Herds Boy, 1985
Oil on plastic
30 × 21 cm
(11 ¾ × 8 ¼ inches)

From The River, 1985
Oil on plastic
30 × 21 cm
(11 ¾ × 8 ¼ inches)

Three Cows, 1985
Oil on Plastic
30 × 21 cm
(11 ¾ × 8 ¼ inches)
Fairholme Collection

A Dream in the World, 1998
Oil on canvas
38 × 26.8 cm
(15 × 10 ½ inches)

Biographies

*Sane Wadu * 1954 in Nyathuna, Kenya*
Sane Wadu started his career in painting in 1983, and is one of the founding members of Ngecha Artist Association. Wadu currently runs, with his wife Eunice Wadu, the Sane Wadu Trust for children's education, where he conducts art workshops, as well as art therapy sessions in prisons and in Naivasha. He has exhibited locally with shows at the Gallery Watatu, Nairobi (1989, 1990, 1995); British Council, 1995); Gallery of East African Contemporary Art (1996, 1999); Red Hill Art Gallery; Alliance Française, Nairobi; and the Rahimtulla Museum of Modern Art. His work has been shown internationally at the Brookes Adobe Arts Center, Santa Barbara (1986); Philippe Briet Gallery, New York (1989); Grafolies, Biennale d'Abidjan (1993); Stadtmuseum Ludwigshafen, Ludwigshafen am Rhein (1993); Parco Art Gallery, Tokyo and Nagoya (1993); Whitechapel Gallery, London (1995); Africus, Johannesburg Biennial (1995); Kunst Transit, Berlin (1999); and The Living Room Gallery, Atlanta (2000). His work sits in collections such as those of Jacques Soulilou and the late Robert Loder of Triangle Network, the collection of Iwalewahaus, Bayreuth, and the Weltkulturen Museum, Frankfurt am Main.

Rosie Olang' Odhiambo
Rosie Olang' Odhiambo is a writer, artist and independent curator based in Nairobi, Kenya. Her current artistic and curatorial interests explore zines, artist's books and other unconventional book structures as formats to play across various disciplines – visual arts, literature, and poetry – engaging with decolonial, queer, feminist, and black radical traditions. Rosie has worked in research, communications, writing, and project management roles with arts and culture organizations in East Africa and the United States. She is the co-founder of MagicDoor, an experimental imprint in Nairobi, and has previously served as the Head of Programs at the Nairobi Contemporary Art Institute (NCAI). In 2022, she participated in the 8th Edition of the Àsìkò School and is a scholar-in-residence at the Indianapolis Museum of Art, Newfields, Indiana.

Mukami Kuria
Mukami Kuria is an almost-barrister, sometimes-art writer, once-in-a-while curator and occasional freelance editor living and working between Nairobi and London. She was the curator of *I Hope So: Sane Wadu* at NCAI in 2022. Under NCAI, she is a co-founder and co-convenor of The Gathering with Michael Armitage and also convened the NCAI Women in Sculpture Panel with Wangechi Mutu, Magdalene Odundo DBE and Chelenge Van Rampelberg on the occasion of the Ledge Sculpture intervention at the Royal Academy of Arts, London. Her editorial projects include *Just A Book*, part of the Contact Zones NRB series, and she has written commissioned texts for *Michael Armitage: The Chapel* at South London Gallery, and for the Goethe Institute Project, Ten Cities.

(facing) Exhibition view, *I Hope So: Sane Wadu* at NCAI, 2022

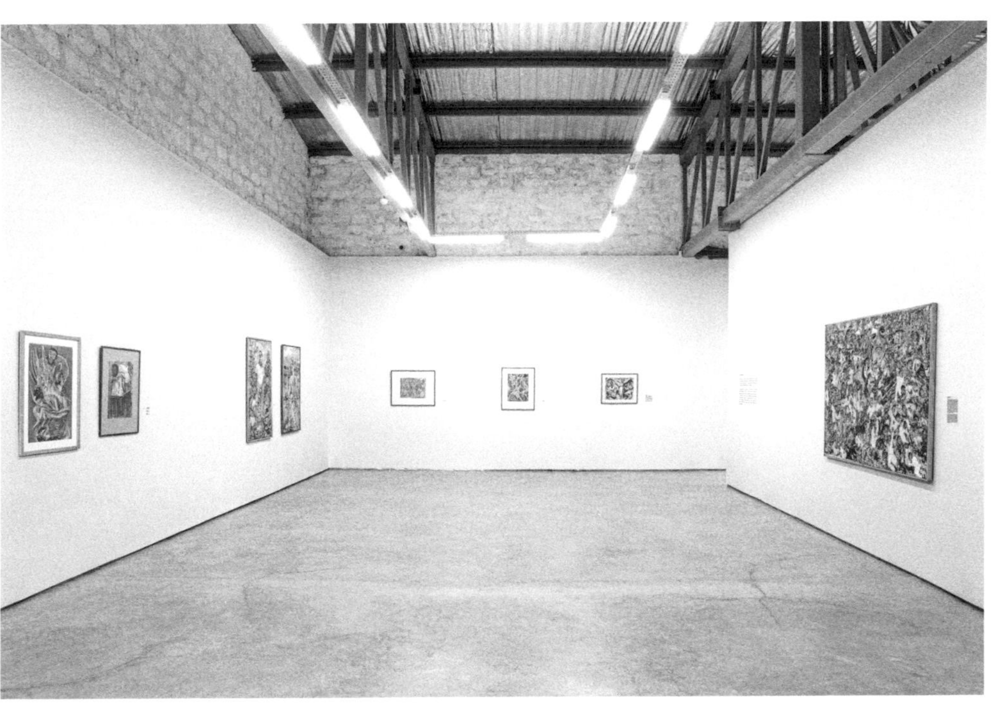

Published by NCAI PUBLICATIONS on the occasion of the exhibition at

Nairobi Contemporary Art Institute
Rosslyn Riviera Mall
3rd Floor
Limuru Rd, Nairobi
Kenya

Coordinated by Nasrin Leahy
Edited by Wairimu Muriithi and Otieno Owino
Designed by Studio Mathias Clottu

Contributors
Mukami Kuria
Rosie Olang' Odhiambo
Sane Wadu

Photography
James Muriuki
Tahir Karmali (installation view)

Lenders
Sane Wadu
Fairholme Collection

Printed by DZA Druckerei zu Altenburg, Germany
ISBN 978-9914-9625-5-0

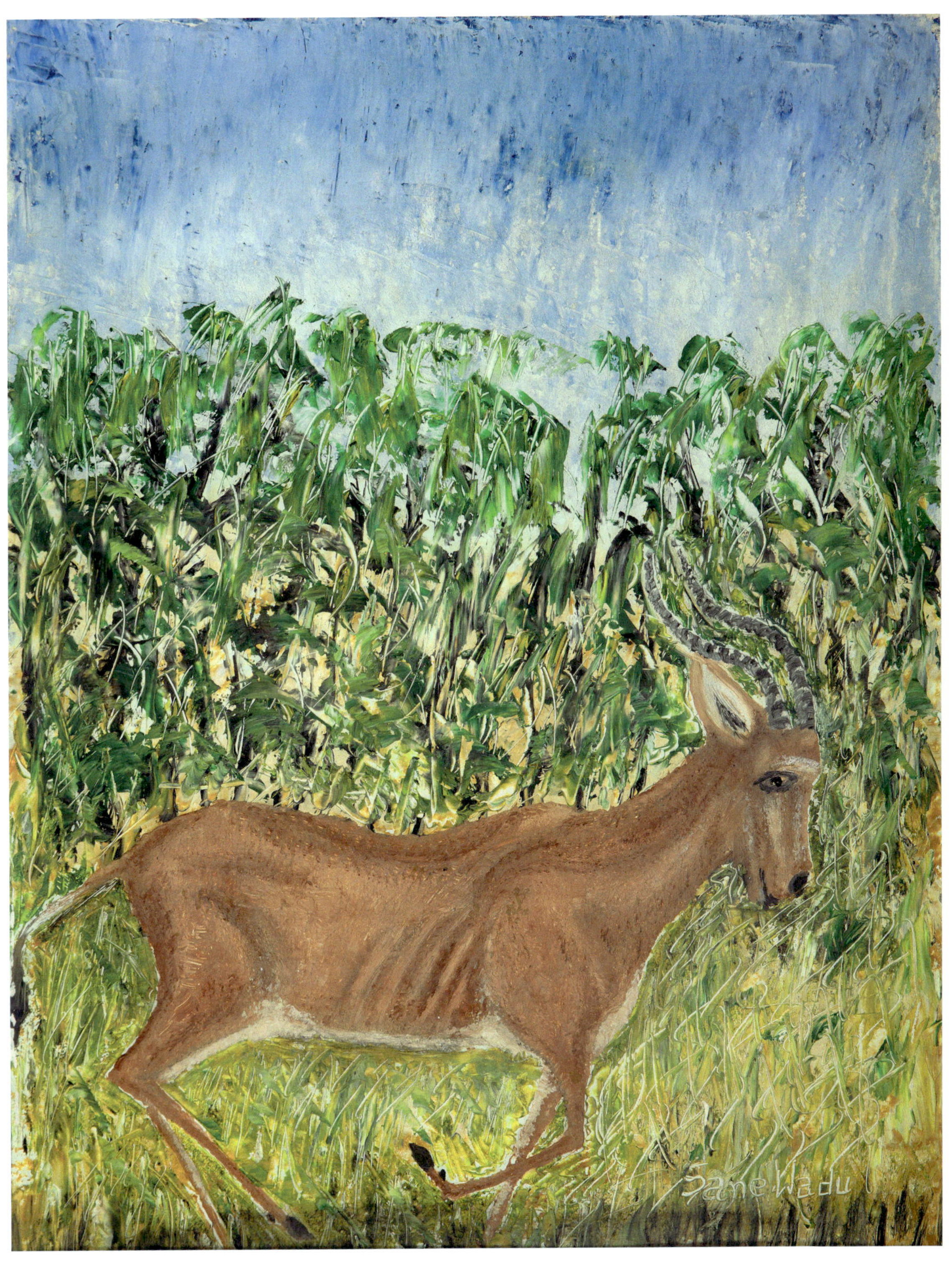

49 Antelope *following spread* Ants Bear

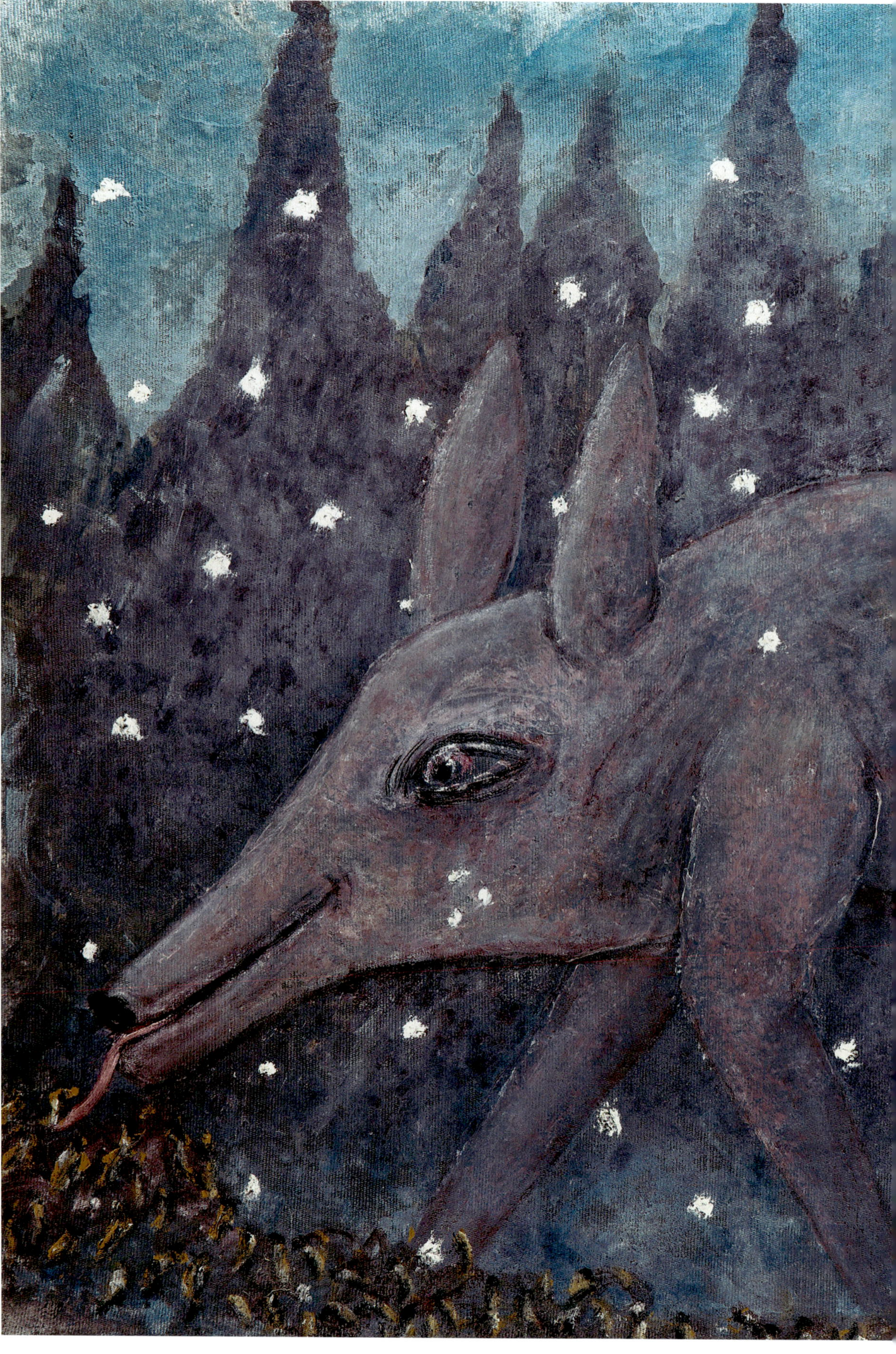

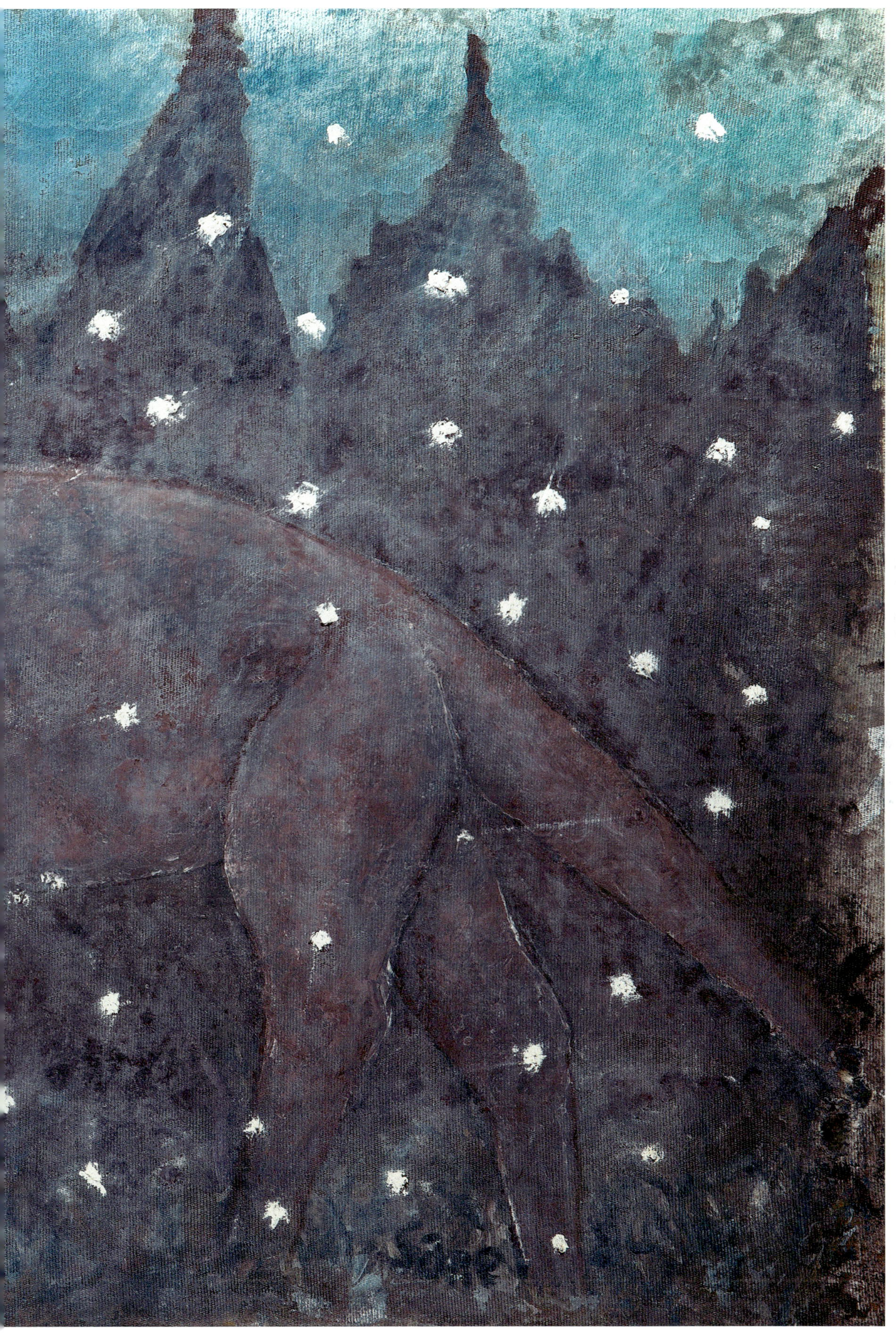

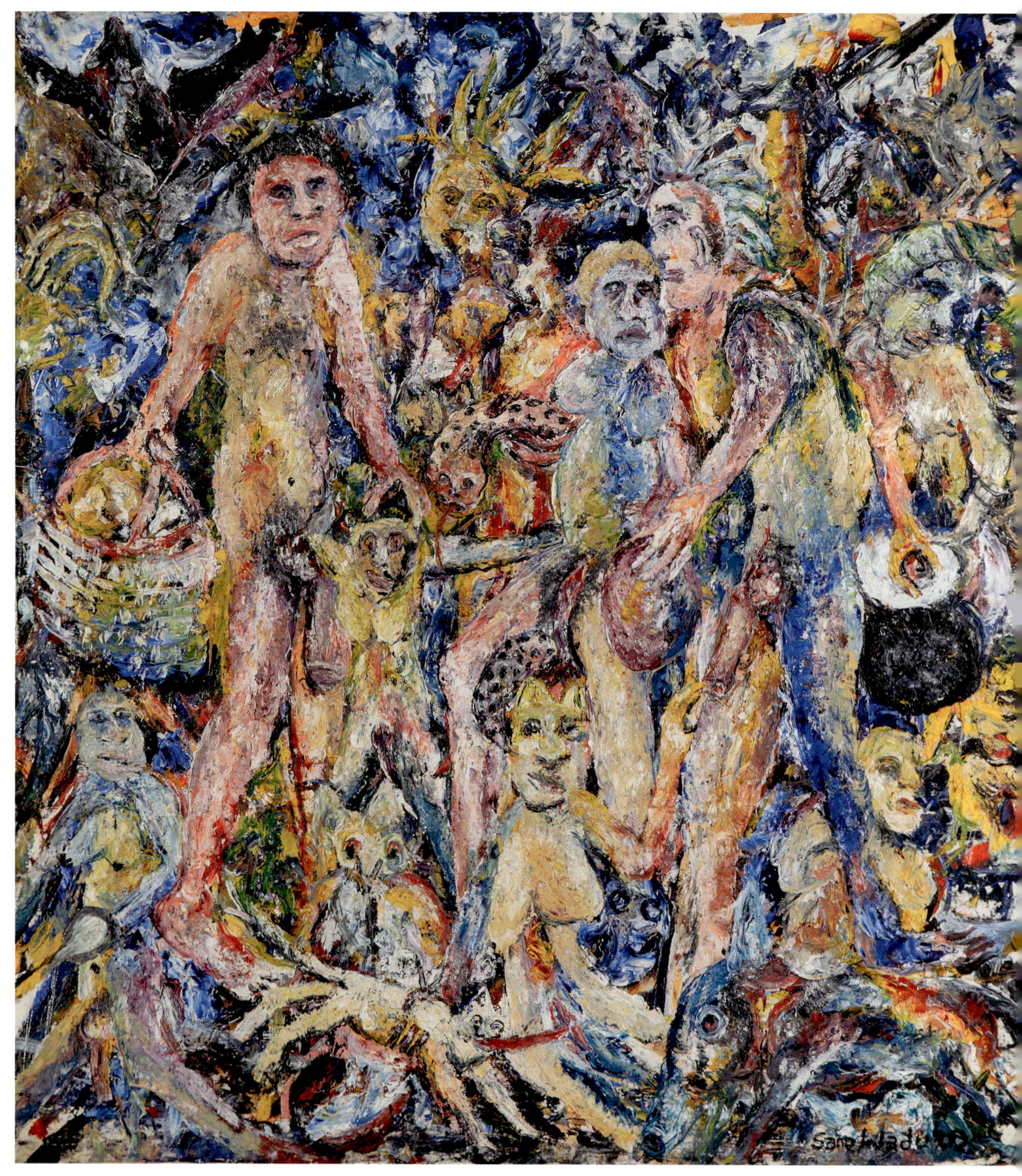

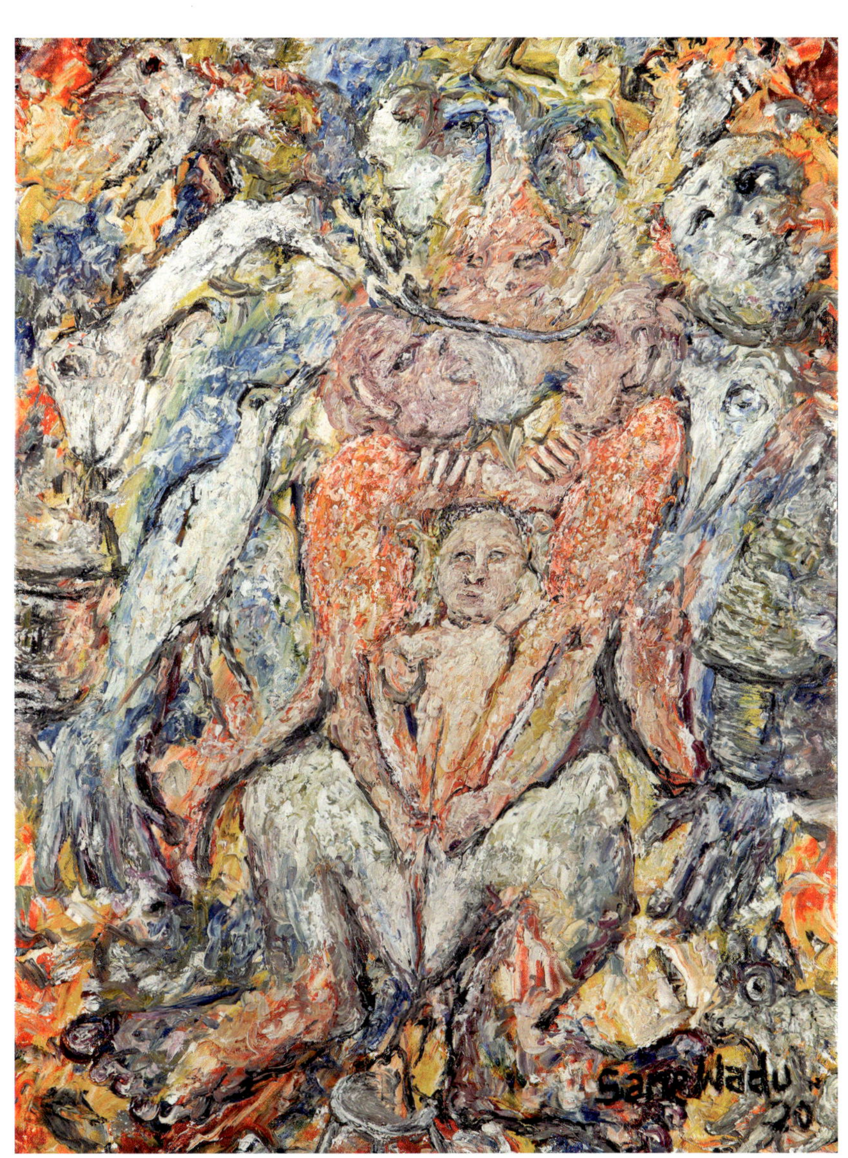
Sane Wadu
20

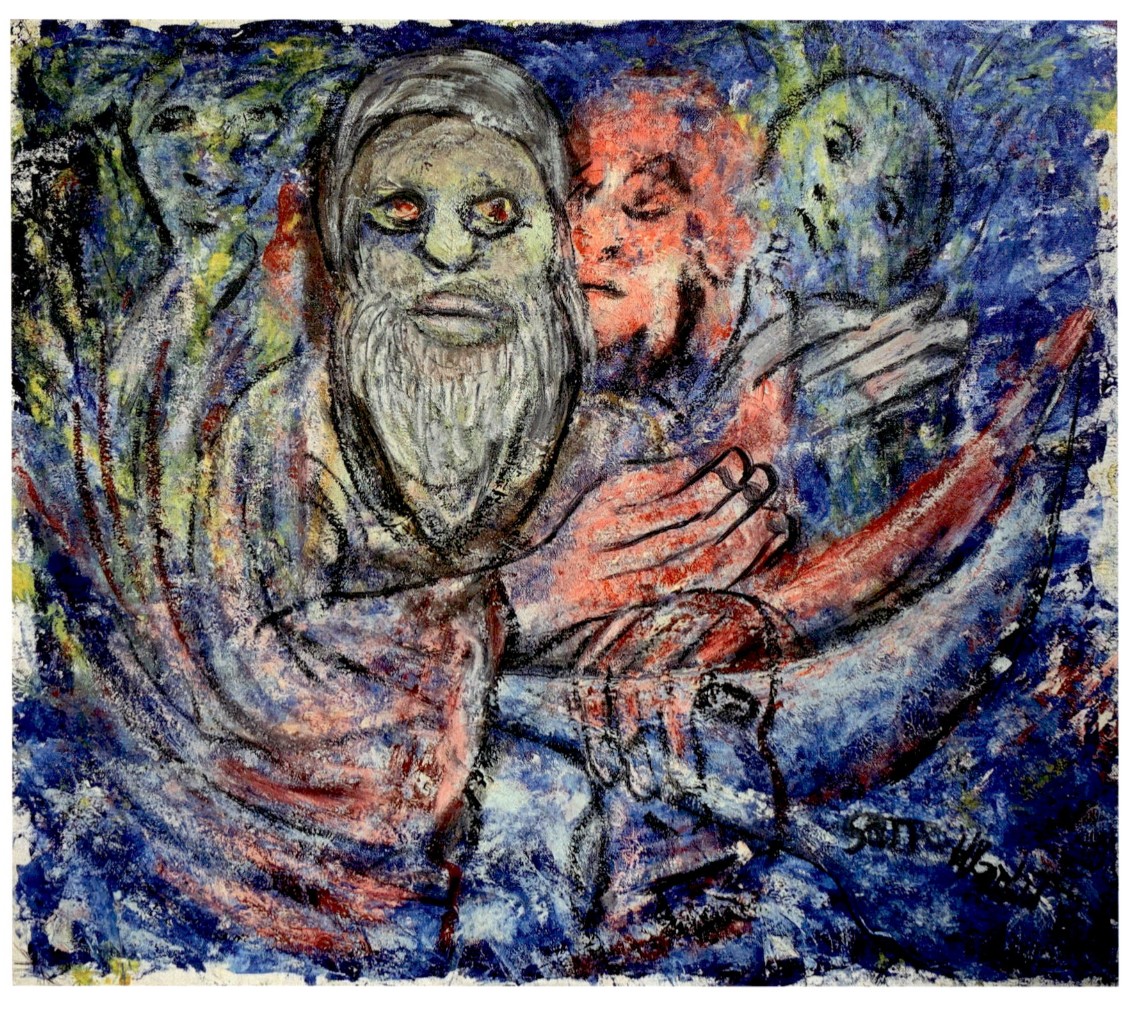

 A Pope *and* Long Legs (Things Men Do)   *following spread* Black Moses

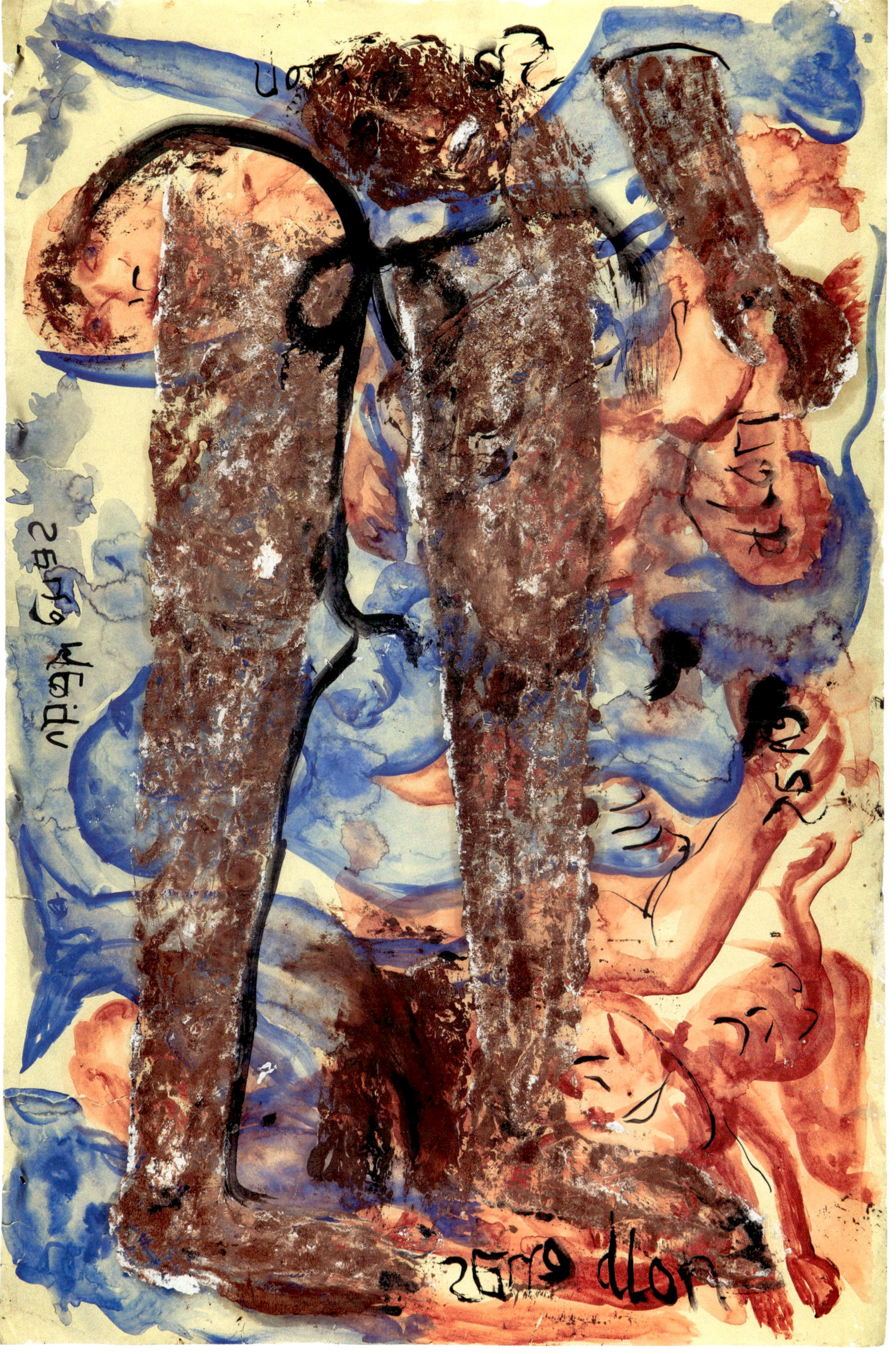

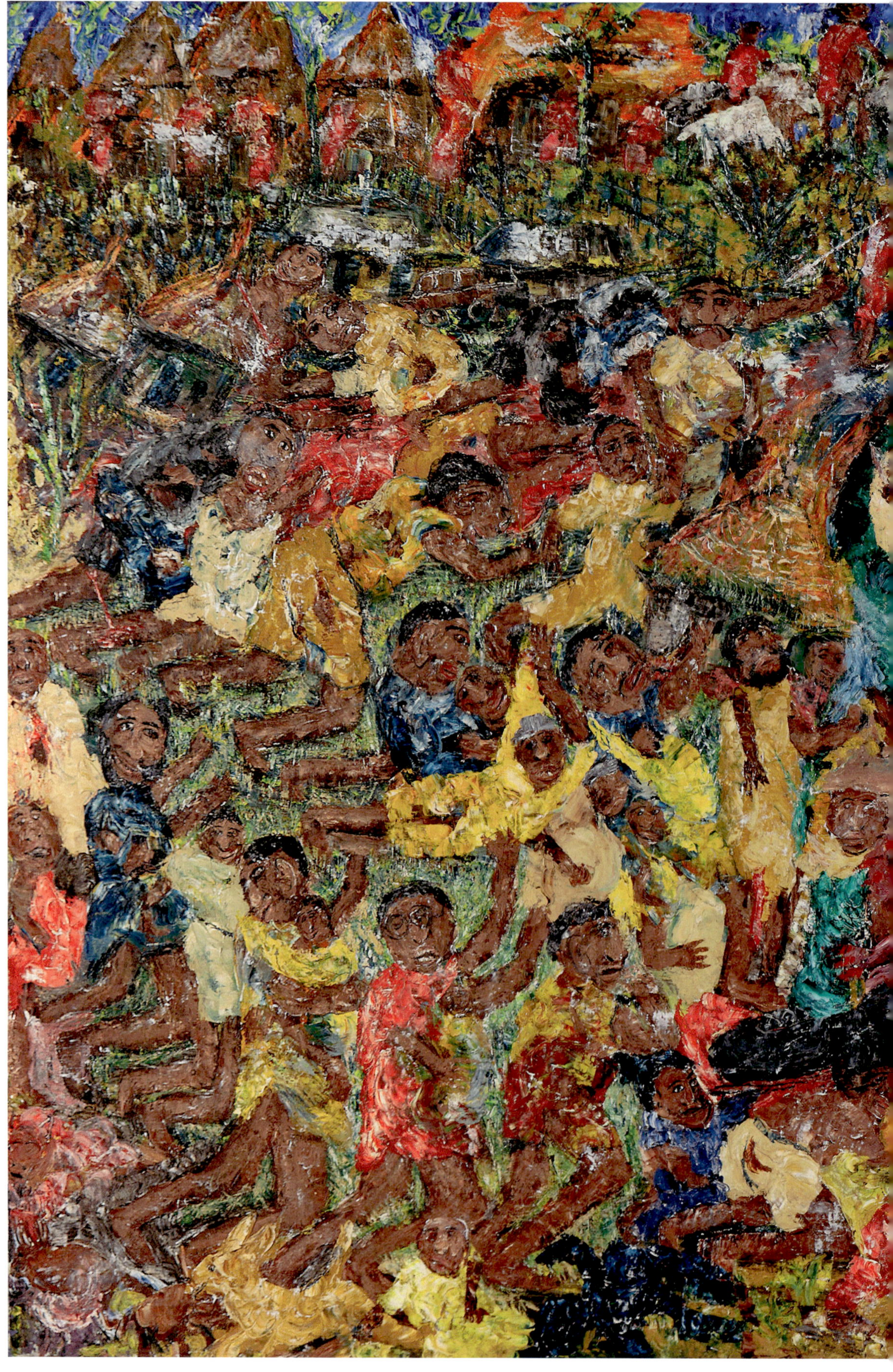

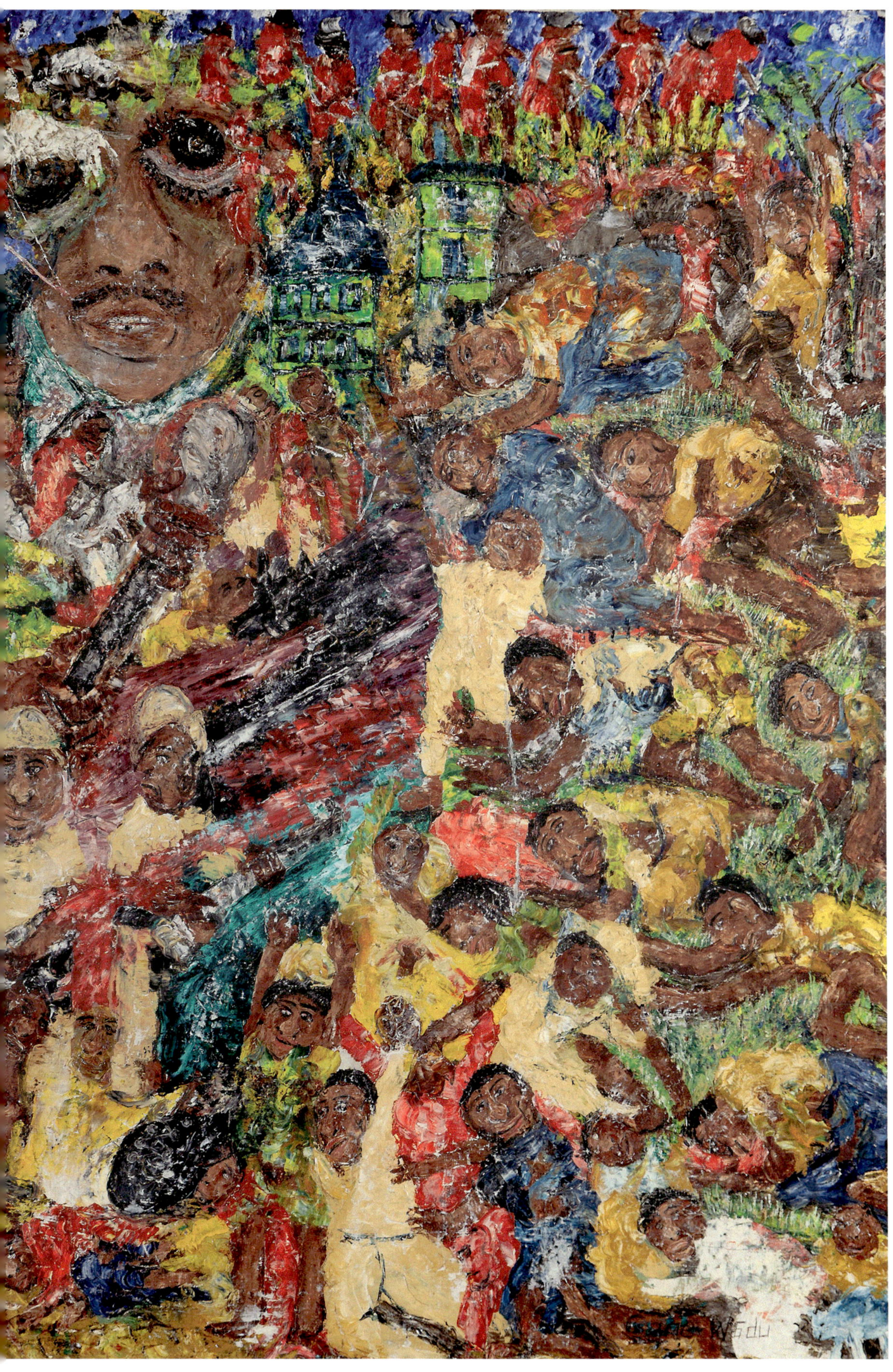

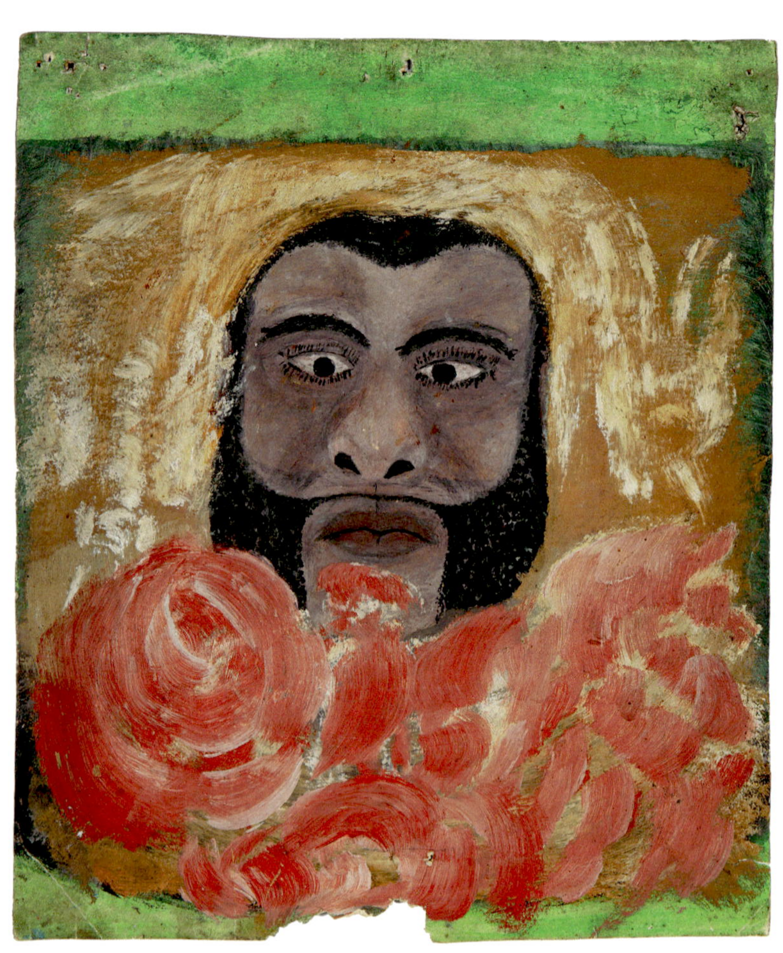

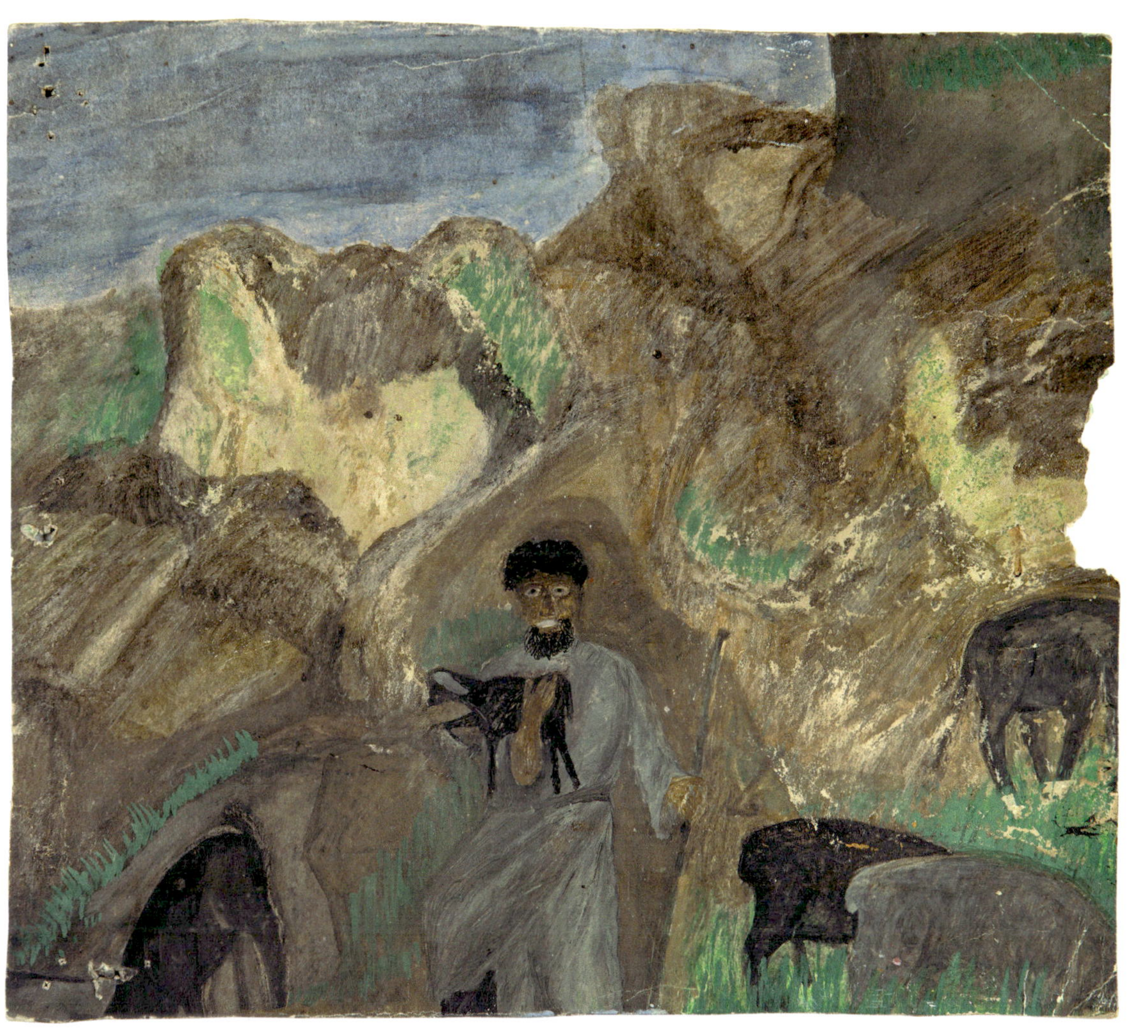

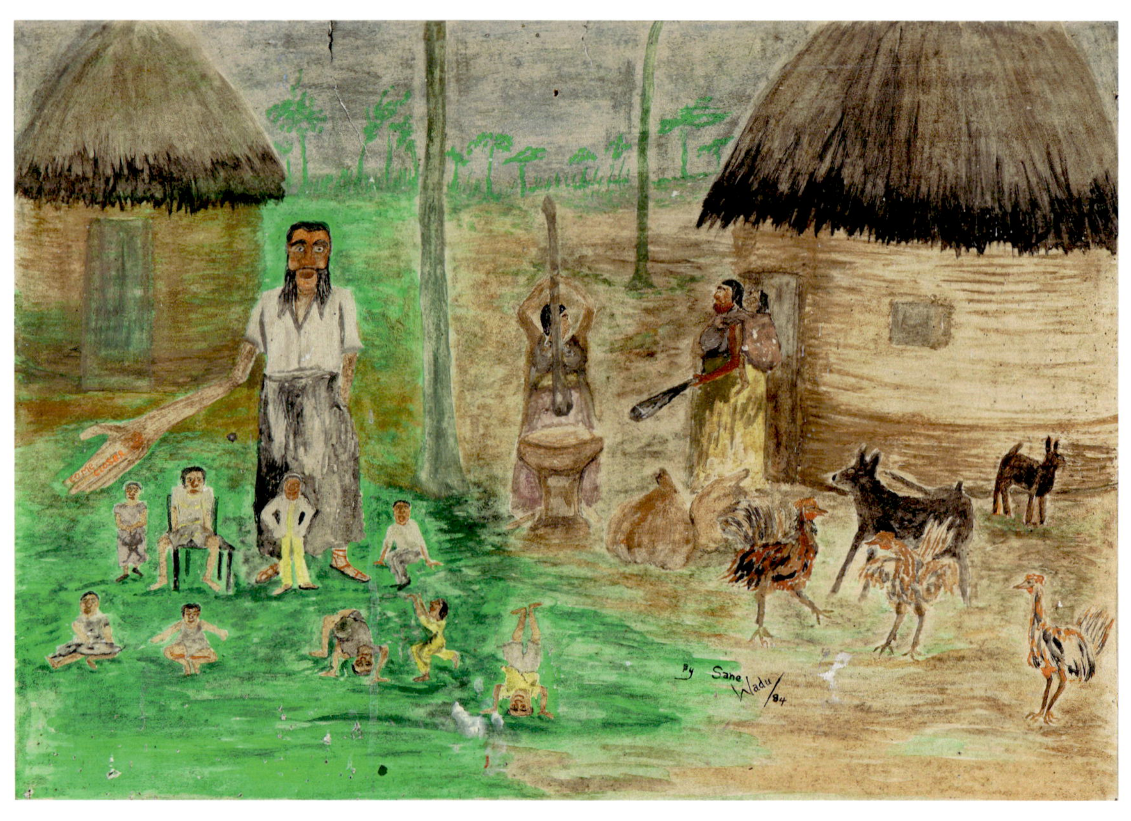
By Sane Wadu/84

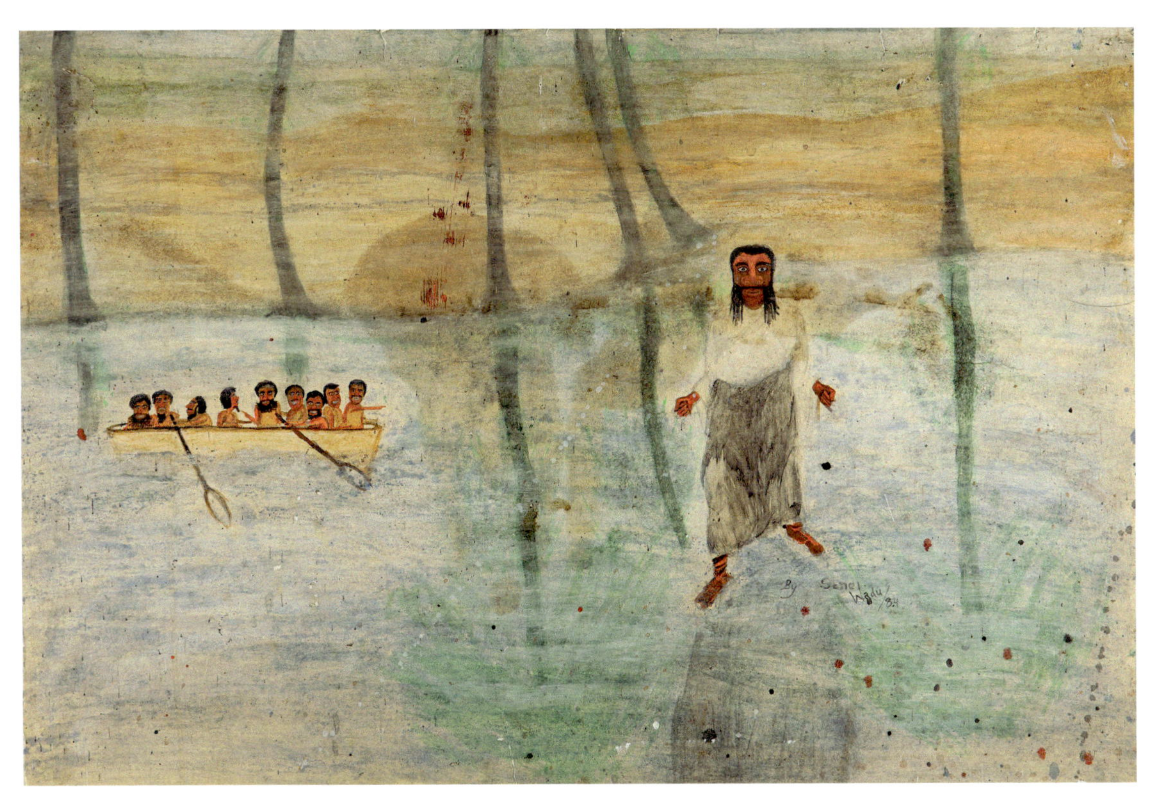
By Sane1 Wadu/84

 preceding spread Come Closer *and* A Walk on Water

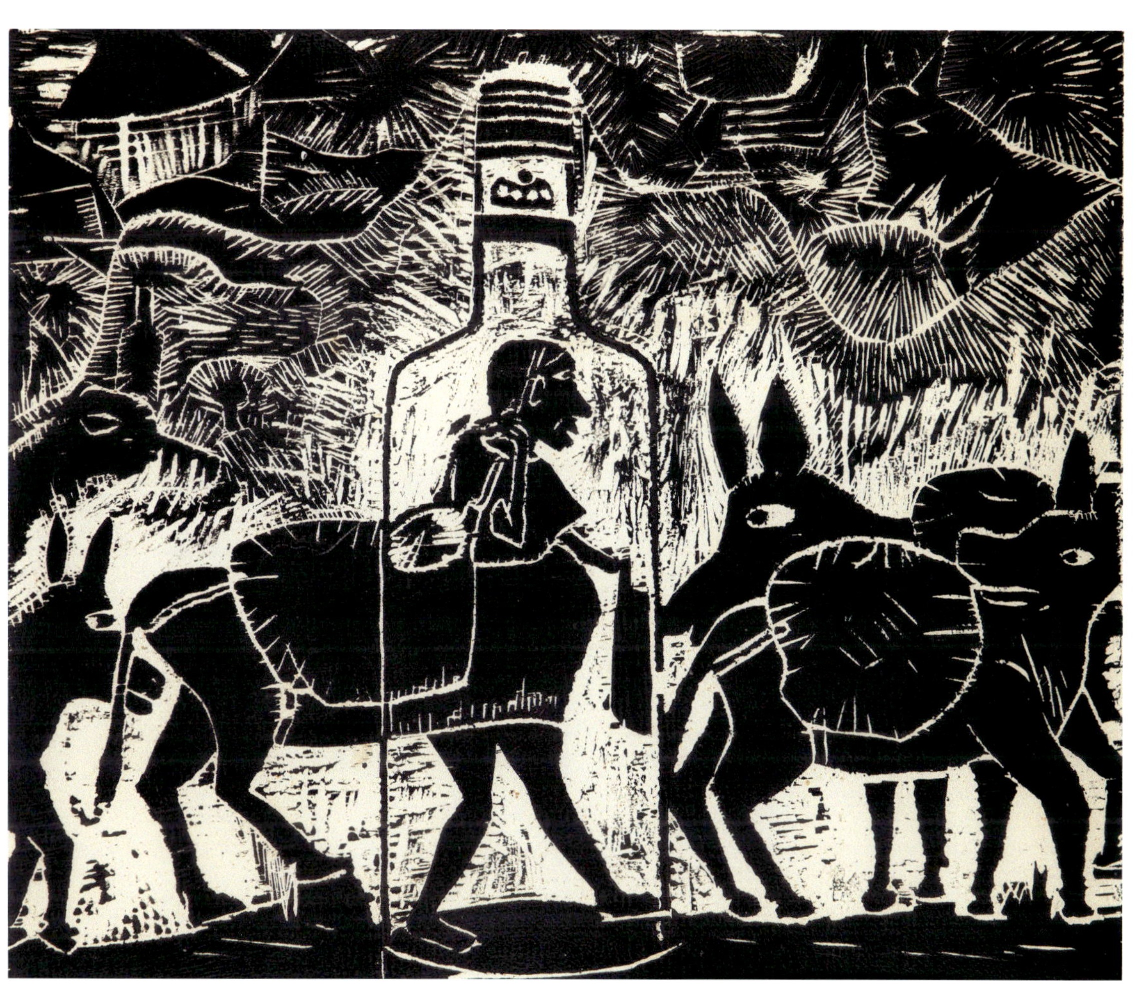

64 My House Gallery *(above) and* Eunice *(below)*

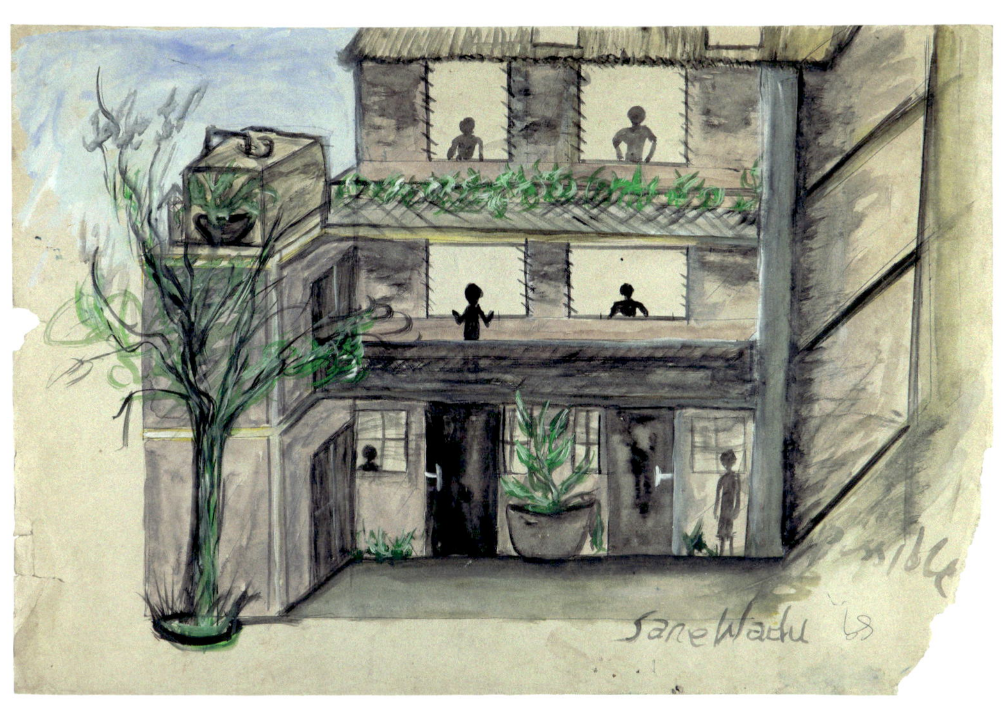
Sane Wadu '68

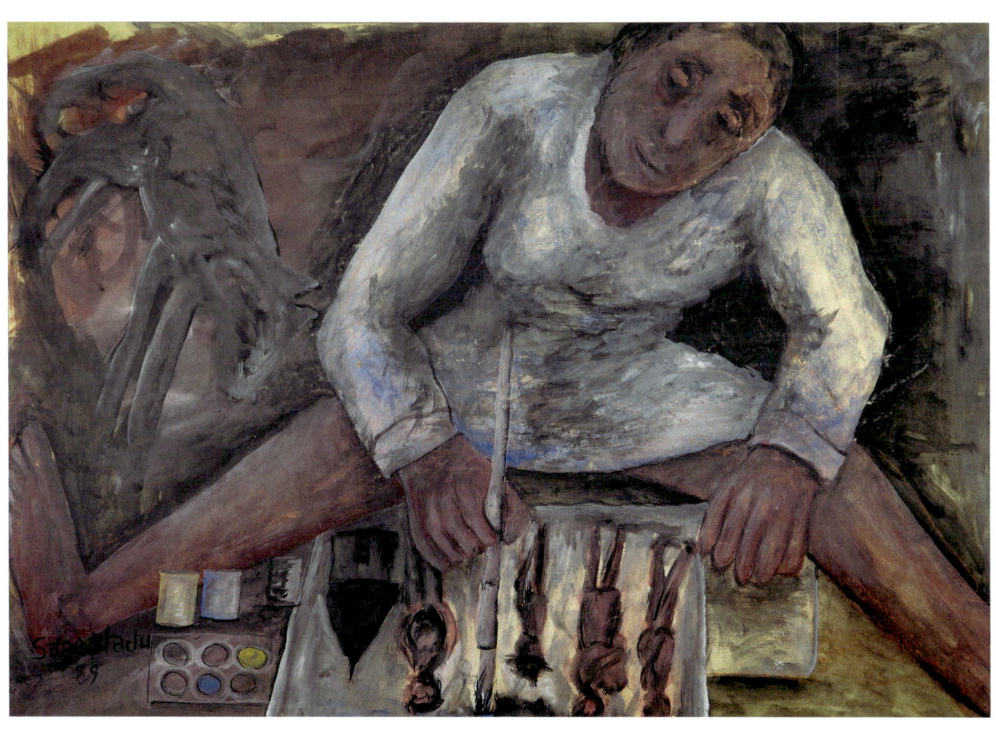

 following spread Herds boy *and* From The River

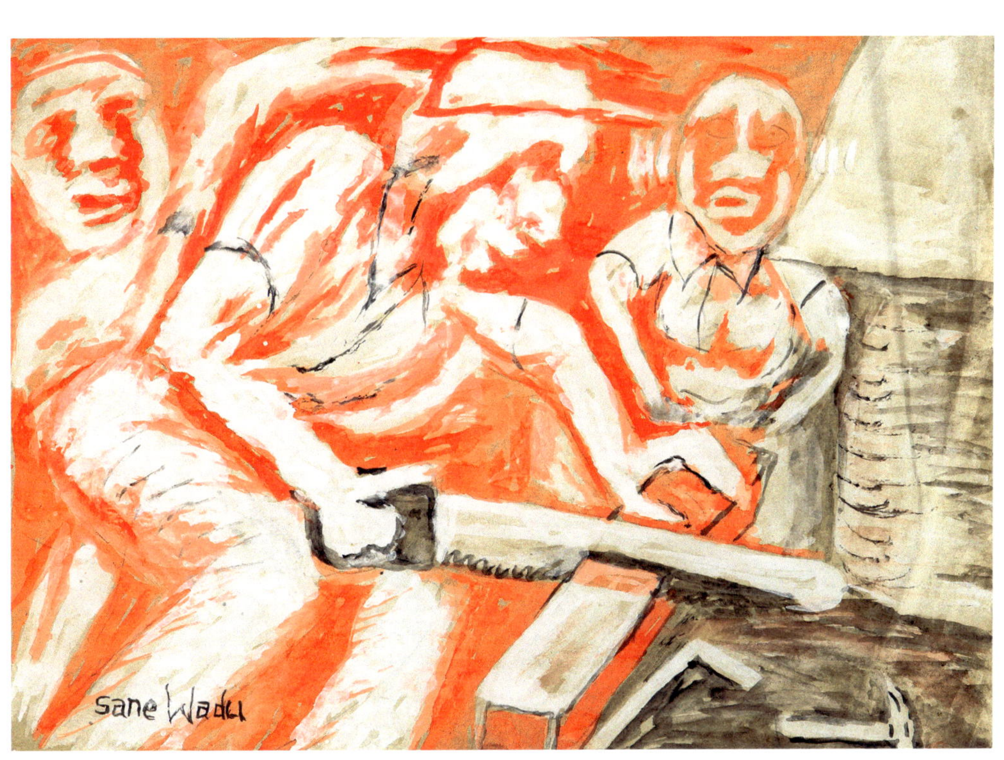
sane Wadu

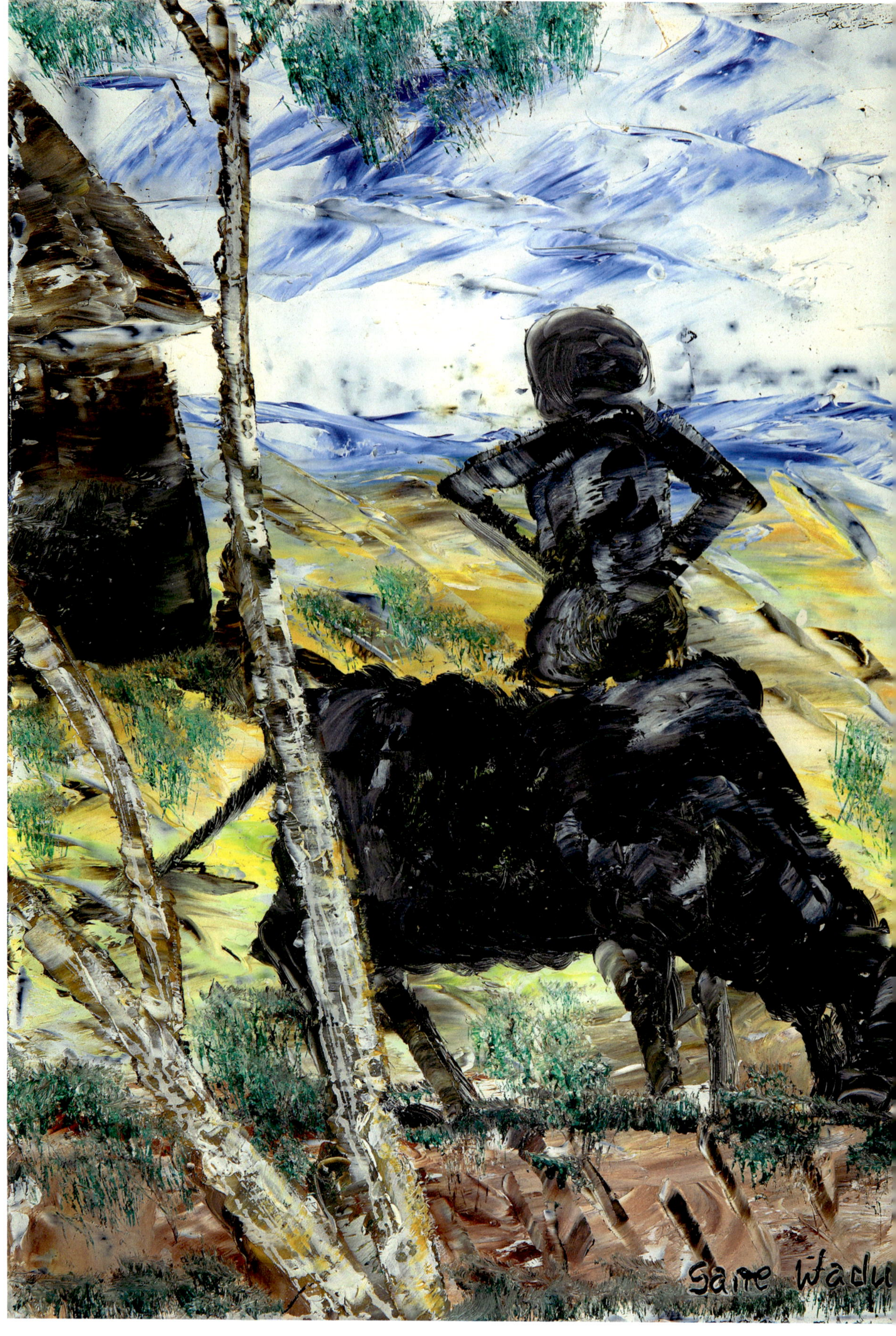
Sane Wadu

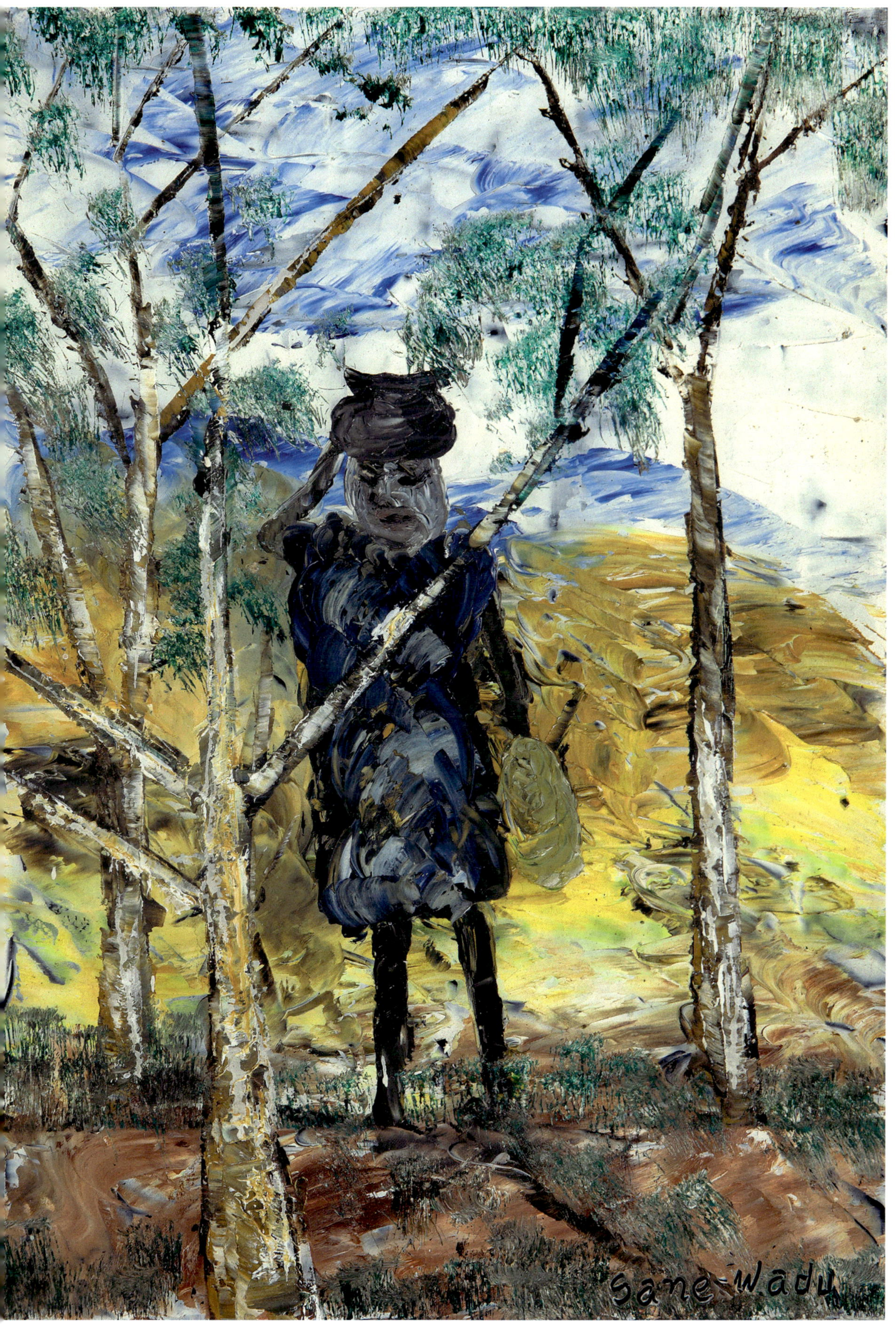
Sane-Wadu

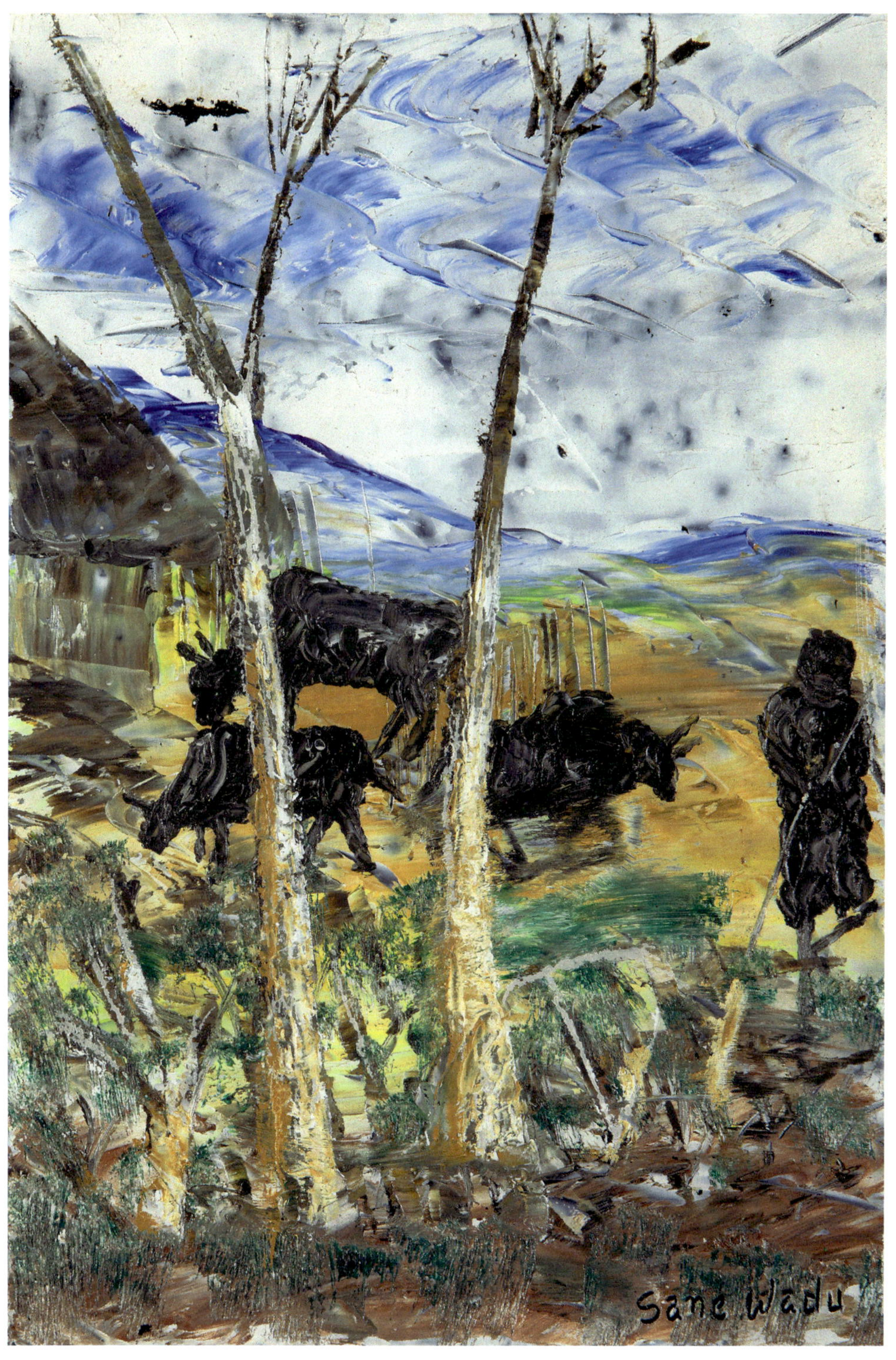
Sane Wadu

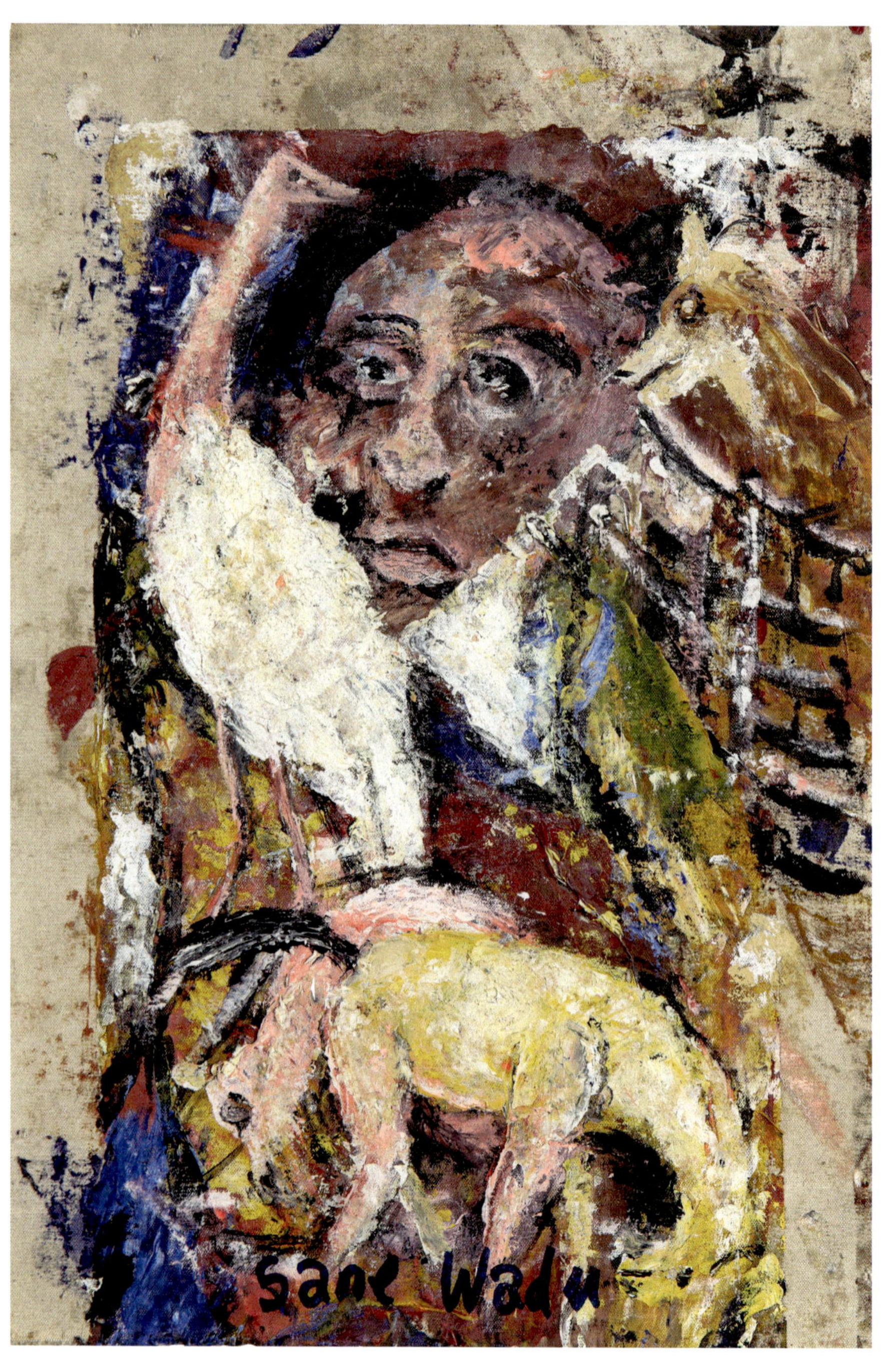
Sane Wadu